D0047744

The
Wiersbe
BIBLE STUDY SERIES

The
Wiersbe
BIBLE STUDY SERIES

2 CORINTHIANS

God Can

Turn Your Trials

into Triumphs

David C Cook®
transforming lives together

THE WIERSBE BIBLE STUDY SERIES: 2 CORINTHIANS
Published by David C Cook
4050 Lee Vance View
Colorado Springs, CO 80918 U.S.A.

David C Cook Distribution Canada
55 Woodslee Avenue, Paris, Ontario, Canada N3L 3E5

David C Cook U.K., Kingsway Communications
Eastbourne, East Sussex BN23 6NT, England

The graphic circle C logo is a registered trademark of David C Cook.

ISBN 978-0-7814-0841-7
eISBN 978-1-4347-0518-1

The Team: Steve Parolini, Karen Lee-Thorp, Amy Konyndyk,
Nick Lee, Jack Campbell, Karen Athen
Series Cover Design: John Hamilton Design
Cover Photo: Veer Inc.

Printed in the United States of America
First Edition 2012

1 2 3 4 5 6 7 8 9 10

082712

Contents

Introduction to 2 Corinthians

Ups and Downs

"You seem to imagine that I have no ups and downs, but just a level and lofty stretch of spiritual attainment with unbroken joy and equanimity. By no means! I am often perfectly wretched and everything appears most murky."

So wrote the man who was called in his day "The Greatest Preacher in the English-speaking World"—Dr. John Henry Jowett. He pastored leading churches, preached to huge congregations, and wrote best-selling books.

"I am the subject of depressions of spirit so fearful that I hope none of you ever get to such extremes of wretchedness as I go to."

Those words were spoken in a sermon by Charles Haddon Spurgeon, whose marvelous ministry in London made him perhaps the greatest preacher England ever produced.

Encouragement

Discouragement is no respecter of persons. The seasoned saint as well as the beginning believer can suffer periods of discouragement. The mature minister, for that matter, may have more to be discouraged about than the youthful pastor who is just getting started.

The message of 2 Corinthians has been an encouragement to me over the years, and now I want it to be an encouragement to you.

—*Warren W. Wiersbe*

How to Use This Study

This study is designed for both individual and small-group use. We've divided it into eight lessons—each references one or more chapters in Warren W. Wiersbe's commentary *Be Encouraged* (second edition, David C Cook, 2010). While reading *Be Encouraged* is not a prerequisite for going through this study, the additional insights and background Wiersbe offers can greatly enhance your study experience.

The **Getting Started** questions at the beginning of each lesson offer you an opportunity to record your first thoughts and reactions to the study text. This is an important step in the study process as those "first impressions" often include clues about what it is your heart is longing to discover.

The bulk of the study is found in the **Going Deeper** questions. These dive into the Bible text and, along with helpful excerpts from Wiersbe's commentary, help you examine not only the original context and meaning of the verses but also modern application.

Looking Inward narrows the focus down to your personal story. These intimate questions can be a bit uncomfortable at times, but don't shy away from honesty here. This is where you are asked to stand before the mirror of God's Word and look closely at what you see. It's the place to take a good look at yourself in light of the lesson and search for ways in which you can grow in faith.

Going Forward is the place where you can commit to paper those things you want or need to do in order to better live out the discoveries you made in the Looking Inward section. Don't skip or skim through this. Take the time to really consider what practical steps you might take to move closer to Christ. Then share your thoughts with a trusted friend who can act as an encourager and accountability partner.

Finally, there is a brief **Seeking Help** section to close the lesson. This is a reminder for you to invite God into your spiritual-growth process. If you choose to write out a prayer in this section, come back to it as you work through the lesson and continue to seek the Holy Spirit's guidance as you discover God's will for your life.

Tips for Small Groups

A small group is a dynamic thing. One week it might seem like a group of close-knit friends. The next it might seem more like a group of uncomfortable strangers. A small-group leader's role is to read these subtle changes and adjust the tone of the discussion accordingly.

Small groups need to be safe places for people to talk openly. It is through shared wrestling with difficult life issues that some of the greatest personal growth is discovered. But in order for the group to feel safe, participants need to know it's okay *not* to share sometimes. Always invite honest disclosure, but never force someone to speak if he or she isn't comfortable doing so. (A savvy leader will follow up later with a group member who isn't comfortable sharing in a group setting to see if a one-on-one discussion is more appropriate.)

Have volunteers take turns reading excerpts from Scripture or from the commentary. The more each person is involved even in the mundane tasks, the more they'll feel comfortable opening up in more meaningful ways.

The leader should watch the clock and keep the discussion moving. Sometimes there may be more Going Deeper questions than your group can cover in your available time. If you've had a fruitful discussion, it's okay to move on without finishing everything. And if you think the group is getting bogged down on a question or has taken off on a tangent, you can simply say, "Let's go on to question 5." Be sure to save at least ten to fifteen minutes for the Going Forward questions.

Finally, soak your group meetings in prayer—before you begin, during as needed, and always at the end of your time together.

Down, Not Out
(2 CORINTHIANS 1—2)

Before you begin ...
- *Pray for the Holy Spirit to reveal truth and wisdom as you go through this lesson.*
- *Read 2 Corinthians 1—2. This lesson references chapters 1 and 2 in* Be Encouraged. *It will be helpful for you to have your Bible and a copy of the commentary available as you work through this lesson.*

Getting Started

From the Commentary

Discouragement is no respecter of persons. In fact, discouragement seems to attack the successful far more than the unsuccessful; for the higher we climb, the farther down we can fall. We are not surprised then when we read that the great apostle Paul was "pressed out of measure" and "despaired even of life" (2 Cor. 1:8). Great as he was in character and ministry, Paul was human just like the rest of us.

Paul could have escaped these burdens except that he had a call from God (2 Cor. 1:1) and a concern to help people. He had founded the church at Corinth and had ministered there for a year and a half (Acts 18:1–18). When serious problems arose in the church after his departure, he sent Timothy to deal with them (1 Cor. 4:17) and then wrote the letter that we call 1 Corinthians.

—*Be Encouraged*, pages 17–18

1. How can we tell from 2 Corinthians 1—2 that matters got worse in the Corinthian church after Paul wrote 1 Corinthians? Why didn't Paul hurry to Corinth to fix things? What challenges did Paul face as he tried to encourage this church?

More to Consider: Before 2 Corinthians was written, Paul wrote a "severe" letter to the church. It was delivered by his associate Titus (2 Cor. 2:4–9; 7:8–12). What might the contents of this severe letter have been? Why might it have caused such distress in the church? What does the existence of this letter reveal about the Corinthian church? About Paul?

2. Choose one verse or phrase from 2 Corinthians 1—2 that stands out to you. This could be something you're intrigued by, something that makes you uncomfortable, something that puzzles you, something that resonates with you, or just something you want to examine further. Write that here.

1:4 He comforts us in all our troubles so that we can comfort others. When they are troubled, we will be able to give them the same comfort God has given us. The more we suffer, the more comfort God gives us.

Going Deeper

From the Commentary

> Paul wrote 2 Corinthians for several reasons. First, he wanted to encourage the church to forgive and restore the member who had caused all the trouble (2 Cor. 2:6–11). He also wanted to explain his change in plans (2 Cor. 1:15–22) and enforce his authority as an apostle (2 Cor. 4:1–2; 10—12). Finally, he wanted to encourage the church to share in the special "relief offering" he was taking up for the needy saints in Judea (2 Cor. 8—9).
>
> One of the key words in this letter is *comfort* or *encouragement*. The Greek word means "called to one's side to help." … In spite of all the trials he experienced, Paul was able (by the grace of God) to write a letter saturated with encouragement.
>
> —*Be Encouraged*, page 18

3. Go through 2 Corinthians 1:1–11 and underline all the uses of the word *comfort* (both as noun and verb). What does this tell you about Paul's primary concern with the Corinthian church? What was Paul's secret to finding peace when facing pressures and trials? What message did he give the Corinthian church about where they could find encouragement?

God is source of all comfort.

From the Commentary

Paul began his letter with a doxology. He certainly could not sing about his circumstances, but he could sing about the God who is in control of all circumstances.

Praise Him because He is God! You find this phrase "blessed be God" in two other places in the New Testament, in Ephesians 1:3 and 1 Peter 1:3. In Ephesians 1:3 Paul praised God for what He did in the past, when He "chose us in [Christ]" (Eph. 1:4) and blessed us "with all spiritual blessings." In 1 Peter 1:3 Peter praised God for future blessings and "a living hope" (NASB). But in 2 Corinthians Paul praised God for present blessings, for what God was accomplishing then and there.

Praise Him because He is the Father of our Lord Jesus Christ! It is because of Jesus Christ that we can call God "Father" and even approach Him as His children. God sees us in His Son and loves us as He loves His Son (John 17:23). We are "beloved of God" (Rom. 1:7) because we are "accepted in the beloved" (Eph. 1:6).

Praise Him because He is the Father of mercies! To the Jewish people, the phrase *father of* means "originator of." Satan is the father of lies (John 8:44) because lies originated with him. According to Genesis 4:21, Jubal was the father of musical instruments because he originated the pipe and the harp. God is the Father of mercies because all mercy originates with Him and can be secured only from Him.

Praise Him because He is the God of all comfort! The words *comfort* or *consolation* (same root word in the Greek) are repeated ten times in 2 Corinthians 1:1–11. We must not think of *comfort* in terms of "sympathy," because sympathy can weaken us instead of strengthen us. God does not pat us on the head and give us a piece of candy or a toy to distract our attention from our troubles. No, He puts strength into our hearts so we can face our trials and triumph over them. Our English word *comfort* comes from two Latin words meaning "with strength." The Greek word means "to come alongside and help." It is the same word used for the Holy Spirit ("the Comforter") in John 14—16.

—*Be Encouraged*, pages 19–20

4. Why did Paul open his letter with a doxology? What had Paul learned about the role of praise in overcoming trials? How does praise change things?

From the Commentary

There are ten basic words for suffering in the Greek language, and Paul used five of them in this letter. The most frequently used word is *thlipsis,* which means "narrow, confined, under pressure," and in this letter is translated "affliction" (2 Cor. 2:4; 4:17), "tribulation" (2 Cor. 1:4), and "trouble" (2 Cor. 1:4, 8). Paul felt hemmed in by difficult circumstances, and the only way he could look was up.

In 2 Corinthians 1:5–6, Paul used the word *pathíma,* "suffering," which was also used for the sufferings of our Savior (1 Peter 1:11; 5:1). There are some sufferings that we endure simply because we are human and subject to pain; but there are other sufferings that come because we are God's people and want to serve Him.

—*Be Encouraged,* page 21

5. Review 2 Corinthians 1:4, 8–11. What do these passages teach us about trials? How can God use trials for good? Is trouble ever an "accident"? Explain.

From the Commentary

Paul was weighed down like a beast of burden with a load too heavy to bear. But God knew just how much Paul could take, and He kept the situation in control.

We do not know what the specific "trouble" was, but it was great enough to make Paul think he was going to die. Whether it was peril from his many enemies (see Acts 19:21ff.; 1 Cor. 15:30–32), serious illness, or special satanic attack, we do not know; but we do know that God controlled the circumstances and protected His servant. When God puts His children into the furnace, He keeps His hand on the thermostat and His eye on the thermometer (1 Cor. 10:13; 1 Peter 1:6–7). Paul may have despaired of life, but God did not despair of Paul.

The first thing He must do is show us how weak we are in ourselves. Paul was a gifted and experienced servant of God, who had been through many different kinds of trials (see 2 Cor. 4:8–12; 11:23ff.). Surely all of this experience would be sufficient for him to face these new difficulties and overcome them.

—*Be Encouraged*, pages 21–22

6. What does Paul's circumstance teach us about the importance of trusting God rather than our gifts or abilities? How does our weakness reveal God's strength (2 Cor. 12:10)? when we are strong in abrities, we are tempted to do God's work on our own. That can lead to pride.
When we're weak, allowing God to fill us with his power, then we are stronger than we could ever be on our own.

From the Commentary

Paul made it clear that we do not need to experience *exactly* the same trials in order to be able to share God's encouragement. If we have experienced God's comfort, then we can "comfort them which are in any trouble" (2 Cor. 1:4b). Of course, if we have experienced similar tribulations, they can help us identify better with others and know better how they feel; but our experiences cannot alter the comfort of God. That remains sufficient and efficient no matter what our own experiences may have been.

Later in 2 Corinthians 12, Paul will give us an example of this principle. He was given a "thorn in the flesh"—some kind of physical suffering that constantly buffeted him. We do not know what this thorn in the flesh was, nor do we need to know. What we do know is that Paul experienced the grace of God and then shared that encouragement with us. No matter what your trial may be, "My grace is sufficient for thee" (2 Cor. 12:9) is a promise you can claim. We would not have that promise if Paul had not suffered.

—*Be Encouraged*, page 25

7. Why is human suffering so hard to understand? What does suffering teach us about the mystery of God? What are some of the different reasons we suffer? How can it help us grow? (See Rom. 5:1–5.) How can it help us share God's character? (See Heb. 12:1–11.)

How does suffering make us grow?
Develops endurance, strength character, deepen trust in God, give greater confidence about future, develop patience.

From the Commentary

> Our English word *conscience* comes from two Latin words: *com*, meaning "with," and *scire*, meaning "to know." Conscience is that inner faculty that "knows with" our spirit and approves when we do right, but accuses when we do wrong. Conscience is not the law of God, but it bears witness to that law. It is the window that lets in the light; and if the window gets dirty because we disobey, then the light becomes dimmer and dimmer (see Matt. 6:22–23; Rom. 2:14–16).

> Paul used the word *conscience* twenty-three times in his letters and spoken ministry as given in Acts. "And herein do I exercise myself, to have always a conscience void to offense toward God, and toward men" (Acts 24:16). When a person has a good conscience, he has integrity, not duplicity; and he can be trusted.

> —*Be Encouraged*, page 32

8. Review 2 Corinthians 1:12–24. How does Paul's use of *conscience* relate to his understanding of the Holy Spirit? What are the differences between a modern understanding of conscience and what Paul was writing about?

More to Consider: Read the following passages: Romans 15:30–32; Ephesians 6:18–19; Philippians 1:19; Colossians 4:3; 1 Thessalonians 5:25; 2 Thessalonians 3:1; Philemon verse 22. What do these verses teach us about Paul? About the importance he placed on prayer? What can we glean from Paul's prayer life that we can apply to our everyday lives?

From the Commentary

> One of the members of the Corinthian church caused Paul a great deal of pain. We are not sure if this is the same man Paul wrote about in 1 Corinthians 5, the man who was living in open fornication, or if it was another person, someone who publicly challenged Paul's apostolic authority. Paul had made a quick visit to Corinth to deal with this problem (2 Cor. 12:14; 13:1) and had also written a painful letter to them about the situation.
>
> —*Be Encouraged*, pages 35–36

9. Review 2 Corinthians 2:1–11. How did Paul reveal a compassionate heart in the way he dealt with the church member who caused him pain? What does this teach us about how we ought to respond to those who hurt us? How can church leadership benefit from Paul's example?

Forgiveness, acceptance, comfort restoration

There is a time to confront and a time to comfort.

From the Commentary

It appeared in Asia that Paul's plans had completely fallen apart. Where was Titus? What was going on at Corinth? Paul had open doors of ministry at Troas, but he had no peace in his heart to walk through those doors. Humanly speaking, it looked like the end of the battle, with Satan as the victor.

Except for one thing: Paul had a conquering faith! He was able to break out in praise and write, "Thanks be unto God" (2 Cor. 2:14). This song of praise was born out of the assurances Paul had because he trusted the Lord.

—Be Encouraged, page 39

10. How did Paul reveal his conquering faith? (See 2 Cor. 2:12–17.) What assurances did Paul have? How are these assurances true for us today?

Looking Inward

Take a moment to reflect on all that you've explored thus far in this study of 2 Corinthians 1—2. Review your notes and answers and think about how each of these things matters in your life today.

> *Tips for Small Groups: To get the most out of this section, form pairs or trios and have group members take turns answering these questions. Be honest and as open as you can in this discussion, but most of all, be encouraging and supportive of others. Be sensitive to those who are going through particularly difficult times and don't press for people to speak if they're uncomfortable doing so.*

11. Paul was able to praise God in the midst of challenging circumstances. Do you praise God when things are tough? Why or why not? What prompts you to praise God? How can you become more able to genuinely praise God in all circumstances?

12. Think about the last time you felt discouraged in your faith. What led to that season of discouragement? What can you take from Paul's story to help you better handle discouragement the next time it comes?

13. How do you see God when you are in the middle of suffering? How easy is it for you to reach out to God when you're suffering? Where does God reveal Himself to you in your suffering?

Going Forward

14. Think of one or two things that you have learned that you'd like to work on in the coming week. Remember that this is all about quality, not quantity. It's better to work on one specific area of life and do it well than to work on many and do poorly (or to be so overwhelmed that you simply don't try).

Do you want to learn how to better handle discouragement? Be specific. Go back through 2 Corinthians 1—2 and put a star next to the phrase or verse that is most encouraging to you. Consider memorizing this verse.

Real-Life Application Ideas: In his letters Paul often asked for people to pray for him. All church leaders need prayer. This week, take some time to pray for each of those leaders in your church and small group. Ask God to give wisdom and grant peace to them. And don't forget to pray for yourself as well. You are a leader to others in some aspect of life, whether you know it or not.

Seeking Help

15. Write a prayer below (or simply pray one in silence), inviting God to work on your mind and heart in those areas you've noted in the Going Forward section. Be honest about your desires and fears.

Notes for Small Groups:

- *Look for ways to put into practice the things you wrote in the Going Forward section. Talk with other group members about your ideas and commit to being accountable to one another.*

- *During the coming week, ask the Holy Spirit to continue to reveal truth to you from what you've read and studied.*

- *Before you start the next lesson, read 2 Corinthians 3. For more in-depth lesson preparation, read chapter 3, "From Glory to Glory," in* Be Encouraged.

Glory
(2 CORINTHIANS 3)

Before you begin …
- *Pray for the Holy Spirit to reveal truth and wisdom as you go through this lesson.*
- *Read 2 Corinthians 3. This lesson references chapter 3 in* Be Encouraged. *It will be helpful for you to have your Bible and a copy of the commentary available as you work through this lesson.*

Getting Started

From the Commentary

Wherever you find the genuine, you will find somebody promoting the counterfeit. Even art critics have been fooled by fake "masterpieces," and sincere publishers have purchased "valuable manuscripts," only to discover them to be forgeries. Henry Ward Beecher was right when he said, "A lie always needs a truth for a handle to it."

No sooner did the gospel of God's grace begin to spread

among the Gentiles than a counterfeit "gospel" appeared, a mixture of law and grace. It was carried by a zealous group of people we have come to call the "Judaizers." Paul wrote his letter to the Galatians to refute their doctrines, and you will find him referring to them several times in 2 Corinthians.

Their major emphasis was that salvation was by faith in Christ *plus* the keeping of the law (see Acts 15:1ff.). They also taught that the believer is perfected in his faith by obeying the law of Moses. Their "gospel of legalism" was very popular, since human nature enjoys achieving religious goals instead of simply trusting Christ and allowing the Holy Spirit to work. It is much easier to measure "religion" than true righteousness.

Paul looked on these false teachers as "peddlers" of the Word of God (see 2 Cor. 2:17 NIV), "religious racketeers" who preyed on ignorant people. He rejected their devious methods of teaching the Bible (2 Cor. 4:2) and despised their tendency to boast about their converts (2 Cor. 10:12–18). One reason why the Corinthians were behind in their contribution to the special offering was that the Judaizers had "robbed" the church (2 Cor. 11:7–12, 20; 12:14).

—*Be Encouraged*, pages 45–46

1. Who were the Judaizers? How did Paul begin to address their emphasis on Moses in 2 Corinthians 3? Why was it important for him to do this?

What would have happened to the Corinthian church if Paul hadn't challenged their doctrine?

2. Choose one verse or phrase from 2 Corinthians 3 that stands out to you. This could be something you're intrigued by, something that makes you uncomfortable, something that puzzles you, something that resonates with you, or just something you want to examine further. Write that here.

Going Deeper

From the Commentary

> The Judaizers boasted that they carried "letters of recom-
> mendation" (2 Cor. 3:1 NIV) from the "important people"
> in the Jerusalem church, and they pointed out that Paul
> had no such credentials. It is a sad thing when a person

measures his worth by what people say about him instead of by what God knows about him. Paul needed no credentials from church leaders: his life and ministry were the only recommendations needed.

When God gave the law, He wrote it on tablets of stone, and those tablets were placed in the ark of the covenant. Even if the Israelites could read the two tablets, this experience would not change their lives. The law is an external thing, and people need an *internal* power if their lives are to be transformed. The legalist can admonish us with his "Do this!" or "Don't do that!" but he cannot give us the power to obey. If we do obey, often it is not from the heart—and we end up worse than before!

—Be Encouraged, page 46

3. Review 2 Corinthians 3:1–3. How was Paul's life enough of a recommendation for him? Why did the Judaizers want to discredit Paul? In what ways is the law an external thing? Why does that matter in Paul's story? In ours today?

More to Consider: Read 1 Corinthians 6:9–11. How is this an example of the ministry of grace? How does the ministry of grace change the heart? What are other biblical examples of the power of grace over the law?

From the Commentary

> The test of ministry is changed lives, not press releases or statistics. It is much easier for the legalist to boast, because he can "measure" his ministry by external standards. The believer who patiently ministers by the Spirit of God must leave the results with the Lord. How tragic that the Corinthians followed the boastful Judaizers and broke the heart of the man who had rescued them from judgment.
>
> —*Be Encouraged*, page 47

4. How might the Judaizers have been measuring their ministry success? How was Paul's ministry a challenge to their methods? What are some external standards by which ministry is sometimes measured today?

From Today's World

Today's church is a mixed bag—just as it was in Paul's day. One of the differences today, however, is the prevalence of megachurches. While most churches seem to welcome growth, some seem almost obsessive about it. And as the church grows, so do the infrastructure needs. A successful megachurch understands these challenges and solves them with creative leadership and small groups. But with a quickly growing church, there is always a risk that the church will become more about numbers than the people themselves.

5. Why do megachurches exist? What is the draw that brings so many people together under one roof? What cautions might Paul have had for these churches? What cautions would he have had for churches that aren't growing? How can leaders properly manage church growth without losing sight of the individual's growth?

From the Commentary

> Paul was quick to give the glory to God and not to himself.
> His confidence ("trust") was in God, and his sufficiency
> came from God. Paul was a brilliant and well-educated

man; yet he did not depend on his own adequacy. He
depended on the Lord.

The legalists, of course, told people that any person could
obey the law and become spiritual. A legalistic ministry
has a way of inflating the egos of people. When you
emphasize the grace of God, you must tell people that
they are lost sinners who cannot save themselves. Paul's
testimony was, "But by the grace of God I am what I am"
(1 Cor. 15:10). No one is sufficient of himself to minister
to the hearts of people. That sufficiency can only come
from God.

—*Be Encouraged*, page 47

6. Note the different names Paul used for the old covenant and the new
covenant in 2 Corinthians 3. How did he contrast the two?

From the Commentary

A legalistic ministry brings death. Preachers who major
on rules and regulations keep their congregations under
a dark cloud of guilt, and this kills their joy, power, and

effective witness for Christ. Christians who are constantly measuring each other, comparing "results," and competing with each other soon discover that they are depending on the flesh and not the power of the Spirit. There never was a standard that could transform a person's life, and that includes the Ten Commandments. Only the grace of God, ministered by the Spirit of God, can transform lost sinners into living epistles that glorify Jesus Christ.

Paul's doctrine of the new covenant was not something that he invented for the occasion. As a profound student of the Scriptures, Paul certainly had read Jeremiah 31:27–34, as well as Ezekiel 11:14–21. In the New Testament, Hebrews 8—10 is the key passage to study.

—*Be Encouraged*, page 48

7. In what ways was the old covenant preparation for the new covenant? What did Paul teach about the role of grace in the new covenant? Why might this have been a difficult concept for the Judaizers to agree with?

From the Commentary

Second Corinthians 3:7–11 is the heart of the chapter, and it should be studied in connection with Exodus 34:29–35. Paul did not deny the glory of the old covenant law, because in the giving of the law and the maintaining of the tabernacle and temple services, there certainly was glory. What he affirmed, however, was that the glory of the new covenant of grace was far superior, and he gave several reasons to support his affirmation.

When Moses descended from the mountain, after conversing with God, his face shone with the glory of God. This was a part of the glory of the giving of the law, and it certainly impressed the people.

—*Be Encouraged*, pages 48–49

8. Review 2 Corinthians 3:7–8. What was Paul saying about the new covenant in these verses? How did he structure his argument? Why did he focus on the theme of "glory" in this passage?

From the Commentary

The tense of the verb in 2 Corinthians 3:11 is very important: "what is passing away" (NKJV). Paul wrote at a period in history when the ages were overlapping. The new covenant of grace had come in, but the temple services were still being carried on and the nation of Israel was still living under law. In AD 70, the city of Jerusalem and the temple would be destroyed by the Romans, and that would mark the end of the Jewish religious system.

The Judaizers wanted the Corinthian believers to go back under the law, to "mix" the two covenants. "Why go back to that which is temporary and fading away?" Paul asked. "Live in the glory of the new covenant, which is getting greater and greater." The glory of the law is but the glory of past history, while the glory of the new covenant is the glory of present experience. As believers, we can be "changed ... from glory to glory" (2 Cor. 3:18), something that the law can never accomplish.

The glory of the law was fading in Paul's day, and today that glory is found only in the records in the Bible. The nation of Israel has no temple or priesthood. If they did build a temple, there would be no Shekinah glory dwelling in the Holy of Holies. The law of Moses is a religion with a most glorious past, but it has no glory today. The light is gone; all that remain are shadows (Col. 2:16–17).

—*Be Encouraged*, page 50

9. Why didn't the Judaizers want to adopt the new covenant? Why would it have been hard for them to accept that the old covenant was fading away? What are some reasons why people in church today are often hesitant to deal with positive change?

More to Consider: Read Exodus 34:29–35. Compare this passage to what Paul wrote in 2 Corinthians 3:12–18. How does Paul's metaphor illustrate the openness of the Christian life under grace?

From the Commentary

The lure of legalism is still with us. False cults prey on professed Christians and church members, as did the Judaizers in Paul's day. We must learn to recognize false cults and reject their teachings. But there are also gospel-preaching churches that have legalistic tendencies and keep their members immature, guilty, and afraid. They spend a great deal of time dealing with the externals, and they neglect the cultivation of the inner life. They exalt standards and they denounce sin, but they fail to magnify the Lord Jesus Christ. Sad to say, in some New Testament churches we have an Old Testament ministry.

Paul has now explained two aspects of his own ministry: it is triumphant (2 Cor. 1—2) and it is glorious (2 Cor. 3). The two go together: "Therefore seeing we have this [kind of] ministry, as we have received mercy, we faint not" (2 Cor. 4:1).

—*Be Encouraged*, page 54

10. What are some of the clues that tell us when a so-called church is really a cult? What is the appeal of cults today? Why is legalism still a draw for so many people?

Looking Inward

Take a moment to reflect on all that you've explored thus far in this study of 2 Corinthians 3. Review your notes and answers and think about how each of these things matters in your life today.

Tips for Small Groups: To get the most out of this section, form pairs or trios and have group members take turns answering these questions. Be honest and as open as you can in this discussion, but most of all, be encouraging and supportive of others. Be sensitive to those who are going through particularly difficult times and don't press for people to speak if they're uncomfortable doing so.

11. Where are you in the "law versus grace" conversation? Do you tend to accept grace, or do you long for the structure of the law? What appeals to you about the new covenant? What role do you think rules should play in the Christian life? What does living by grace look like for you in practice?

12. Have you ever felt more like a number on a membership roll than a person when in church? Explain. How would you like your church to measure success? What role can you have in that? How does this line up with what Paul taught in 2 Corinthians?

13. Have you ever visited a cult-like church or been a part of a church you'd consider to be a cult? What drew you to that organization? Why did you leave? What are some practical ways to protect yourself from the dangers of legalism and other cultic practices?

Going Forward

14. Think of one or two things that you have learned that you'd like to work on in the coming week. Remember that this is all about quality, not quantity. It's better to work on one specific area of life and do it well than to work on many and do poorly (or to be so overwhelmed that you simply don't try).

Do you want to live more by grace? Be specific. Go back through 2 Corinthians 3 and put a star next to the phrase or verse that is most encouraging to you. Consider memorizing this verse.

Real-Life Application Ideas: Paul's challenges in dealing with the Corinthians were to a great degree due to the Judaizers and their insistence on maintaining a legalistic approach to their faith. Take time this week to evaluate your own faith habits. In what ways are you living under grace? How are you still holding on to legalism? Then consider what it would look like to let go of your legalistic tendencies and accept grace in those areas of life. This is much harder than it seems, so it might be good to share your journey with a mentor or small-group leader who can provide another perspective.

Seeking Help

15. Write a prayer below (or simply pray one in silence), inviting God to work on your mind and heart in those areas you've noted in the Going Forward section. Be honest about your desires and fears.

Notes for Small Groups:

- *Look for ways to put into practice the things you wrote in the Going Forward section. Talk with other group members about your ideas and commit to being accountable to one another.*

- *During the coming week, ask the Holy Spirit to continue to reveal truth to you from what you've read and studied.*

- *Before you start the next lesson, read 2 Corinthians 4—5. For more in-depth lesson preparation, read chapters 4 and 5, "Courage for the Conflict" and "Motives for Ministry," in* Be Encouraged.

Courage and Motives

(2 CORINTHIANS 4—5)

Before you begin …
- *Pray for the Holy Spirit to reveal truth and wisdom as you go through this lesson.*
- *Read 2 Corinthians 4—5. This lesson references chapters 4 and 5 in* Be Encouraged. *It will be helpful for you to have your Bible and a copy of the commentary available as you work through this lesson.*

Getting Started

From the Commentary

"Therefore, seeing we have *this kind* of ministry" is the literal translation of what Paul wrote in 2 Corinthians 4:1. What kind of ministry? The kind described in the previous chapter: a glorious ministry that brings men life, salvation, and righteousness; a ministry that is able to transform men's lives. This ministry is a gift—we receive it from God. It is given to us because of God's mercy.

—*Be Encouraged,* page 57

1. Read 1 Timothy 1:12–17. How does this passage describe the ministry Paul talked about in 2 Corinthians 4? How does the way we look at our ministry determine how we'll fulfill it? What does it take to see ministry as a joy and not a begrudging task?

2. Choose one verse or phrase from 2 Corinthians 4—5 that stands out to you. This could be something you're intrigued by, something that makes you uncomfortable, something that puzzles you, something that resonates with you, or just something you want to examine further. Write that here.

Going Deeper

From the Commentary

Paul was certainly alluding to the Judaizers when he wrote the words in 2 Corinthians 4:2. Many false teachers today claim to base their doctrine on the Word of God, but false teachers handle God's Word in deceptive ways. You can prove anything by the Bible, provided you twist the Scriptures out of context and reject the witness of your own conscience. The Bible is a book of literature, and it must be interpreted according to the fundamental rules of interpretation. If people treated other books the way they treat the Bible, they would never learn anything.

Paul had nothing to hide, either in his personal life or in his preaching of the Word. Everything was open and honest; there was no deception or distortion of the Word. The Judaizers were guilty of twisting the Scriptures to fit their own preconceived interpretations, and ignorant people were willing to follow them.

—*Be Encouraged*, pages 58–59

3. What are some ways people twist Scripture today? Why is it easy to twist Scripture? What does this say about the challenges in interpreting Scripture? About the Holy Spirit's role in our understanding God's Word?

More to Consider: Read Romans 11:25 and 2 Corinthians 3:14–16. What do these verses tell us about the minds of the Jews? In what ways are the minds of the Gentiles also blinded?

From the Commentary

The awesome fact that Paul had received this ministry from Christ kept him from being a quitter and a deceiver; but it also kept him from being a self-promoter (2 Cor. 4:5–6). "We preach not ourselves" (2 Cor. 4:5). The Judaizers enjoyed preaching about themselves and glorying in their achievements (2 Cor. 10:12–18). They were not servants who tried to help people; they were dictators who exploited people.

Paul was certainly a man who practiced genuine humility. He did not trust in himself (2 Cor. 1:9) or commend himself (2 Cor. 3:1–5) or preach himself (2 Cor. 4:5). He sought only to lead people to Jesus Christ and to build them up in the faith. It would have been easy for Paul to build a "fan club" for himself and take advantage of weak people who thrive on associating with great men. The Judaizers operated in that way, but Paul rejected that kind of ministry.

What happens when you share Jesus Christ with lost sinners? The light begins to shine! Paul compared conversion to creation as described in Genesis 1:3. Like the earth of Genesis 1:2, the lost sinner is formless and empty; but when he trusts Christ, he becomes a new creation (2 Cor.

5:17). God then begins to *form* and *fill* the life of the person who trusts Christ, and he begins to be fruitful for the Lord. God's "Let there be light!" makes everything new.

—*Be Encouraged*, pages 59–60

4. Review 2 Corinthians 4:4–6. Paul revealed himself as someone who didn't self-promote, and yet it appears at times that he was very sure of himself. How was Paul's confidence different from self-promotion? How could Paul have taken advantage of his status? What did he do instead?

From the Commentary

From the glory of the new creation, Paul moved to the humility of the clay vessel in 2 Corinthians 4:7–12. The believer is simply a "jar of clay"; it is the treasure *within the vessel* that gives the vessel its value. The image of the vessel is a recurring one in Scripture, and from it we can learn many lessons.

To begin with, God has made us the way we are so that we can do the work He wants us to do. God said of Paul, "He is a chosen vessel unto me, to bear my name before the Gentiles" (Acts 9:15). No Christian should ever complain to God because of his lack of gifts or abilities, or because of his limitations or handicaps. Psalm 139:13–16 indicates that our very genetic structure is in the hands of God. Each of us must accept himself and be himself.

—*Be Encouraged*, page 60

5. What's the practical significance of Paul's vessel metaphor? (See 2 Tim. 2:20–21.) Why are we "earthen" vessels? Where does God fit in this metaphor?

From the Commentary

The phrase *spirit of faith* in 2 Corinthians 4:13 means "attitude or outlook of faith." Paul was not referring to a special gift of faith (1 Cor. 12:9), but rather to that attitude of faith that ought to belong to every believer. He saw himself identified with the believer who wrote Psalm 116:10: "I believed, therefore have I spoken." True witness for God is based on faith in God, and this faith comes from God's Word (Rom. 10:17). Nothing closes a believer's mouth like unbelief (see Luke 1:20).

Of what was Paul so confident? That he had nothing to fear from life or death! He had just listed some of the trials that were a part of his life and ministry, and now he was affirming that his faith gave him victory over all of them.

—*Be Encouraged,* page 62

6. What are the assurances Paul listed in 2 Corinthians 4:14–18? How does each of these assurances require faith? If these assurances are guaranteed, what are the implications for the way we live our daily lives?

From the Commentary

"We have this ministry.... We have this treasure.... We [have] the same spirit of faith.... We have a building of God" (2 Cor. 4:1, 7, 13; 5:1). What a testimony Paul gave to the reality of the Christian faith!

This "building of God" is not the believer's heavenly home, promised in John 14:1–6. It is his glorified body.

Paul was a tentmaker (Acts 18:1–3), and here he used a tent as a picture of our present earthly bodies. A tent is a weak, temporary structure, without much beauty; but the glorified body we shall receive will be eternal, beautiful, and never show signs of weakness or decay (see Phil. 3:20–21). Paul saw the human body as an earthen vessel (2 Cor. 4:7) and a temporary tent; but he knew that believers would one day receive a wonderful glorified body, suited to the glorious environment of heaven.

—*Be Encouraged*, page 65

7. Review 2 Corinthians 5:1–8. How does Paul's past life as a tentmaker play into his message here? How are heavenly bodies different from earthly ones? (See Phil. 3:20–21.) Does looking forward to our heavenly bodies mean our current bodies are disposable junk? Explain.

From the Commentary

Paul usually connected *duty* and *doctrine*, because what God has done for us must motivate us to do something for God.

"You would have preached a marvelous sermon," a woman said to her pastor, "except for all those 'therefores' at the end!"

Paul would have agreed with the pastor, for he usually used "therefores" and "wherefores" liberally in his letters. In fact, you find them in this section of 2 Corinthians 5 in verses 9, 11, and 16–17. Paul moved from explanation to application, and his theme was *motivation for ministry*. His enemies had accused him of using the ministry of the gospel for his own selfish purposes, when in reality *they* were the ones who were "merchandising" the gospel (see 2 Cor. 2:17; 4:2).

We must never force people to trust Christ, or coerce them by some devious approach. "Our message to you is true, our motives are pure, our conduct is absolutely aboveboard" (1 Thess. 2:3 PH). The Christian worker must have the right motive for ministry as well as the right message.

—*Be Encouraged*, pages 71–72

8. Phillips Brooks said, "Christianity knows no truth which is not the child of love and the parent of duty." How does this statement line up with Paul's message here? What do 2 Corinthians 5:11 and 5:20 tell us is the ministry of a Christian? Why is motive important to ministry?

More to Consider: The attitude Paul described as the "fear of the Lord" in 2 Corinthians 5:11 is often lacking in ministry. The famous Bible scholar B. F. Westcott once wrote, "Every year makes me tremble at the daring with which people speak of spiritual things." Why is this true today? What accounts for the lack of reverence in the modern church? Where do people offer reverence today? What are some ways today's church can reconnect its members with the idea and practice of reverence?

From the Commentary

Not every believer is ambitious for the Lord, but every believer is going to appear before the Lord; and now is the time to prepare. The judgment seat of Christ is that future event when God's people will stand before the Savior as their works are judged and rewarded (see Rom. 14:8–10). Paul was ambitious for the Lord because he wanted to meet Him with confidence and not shame (1 John 2:28).

The term "judgment seat" comes from the Greek word *bema*, which was the platform in Greek towns where orations were made or decisions handed down by rulers (see Matt. 27:19; Acts 12:21; 18:12). It was also the place where the awards were given out to the winners in the annual Olympic Games. This "judgment seat" must not be confused with the Great White Throne from which Christ will judge the wicked (Rev. 20:11–15). Because of the gracious work of Christ on the cross, believers will not face their sins (John 5:24; Rom. 8:1); but we will have to give an account of our works and service for the Lord.

—*Be Encouraged*, page 73

9. In what ways is the judgment seat a place where things are revealed? What does this suggest about how each Christian ought to consider his or her own life today? What is an example of a "good account" someone might give before Christ?

From the Commentary

The phrase "the love of Christ" means His love for us as seen in His sacrificial death. "We love him, because he first loved us" (1 John 4:19). He loved us when we were unlovely; in fact, He loved us when we were ungodly, sinners, and enemies (see Rom. 5:6–10). When He died on the cross, Christ proved His love for the world (John 3:16), the church (Eph. 5:25), and individual sinners (Gal. 2:20). When you consider the reasons why Christ died, you cannot help but love Him.

The tense of the verb in 2 Corinthians 5:14 gives the meaning "then all died." This truth is explained in detail in Romans 6, the believer's identification with Christ. When Christ died, we died in Him and with Him. Therefore, the old life should have no hold on us today. "I am crucified with Christ" (Gal. 2:20).

In 2 Corinthians 5:15–17, Paul said that Jesus died that we might live. This is the positive aspect of our identification with Christ: we not only died with Him, but we also were raised with Him that we might "walk in newness of life" (Rom. 6:4). Because we have died with Christ, we can overcome sin; and because we live with Christ, we can bear fruit for God's glory (Rom. 7:4).

—*Be Encouraged,* page 76

10. What does it mean to live "through" Jesus? (See 1 John 4:9.) What does it mean to live "for" Him? (See 2 Cor. 5:15.) How do these two ways of living define our ministry?

Looking Inward

Take a moment to reflect on all that you've explored thus far in this study of 2 Corinthians 4—5. Review your notes and answers and think about how each of these things matters in your life today.

Tips for Small Groups: To get the most out of this section, form pairs or trios and have group members take turns answering these questions. Be honest and as open as you can in this discussion, but most of all, be encouraging and supportive of others. Be sensitive to those who are going through particularly difficult times and don't press for people to speak if they're uncomfortable doing so.

11. Do you consider your ministry mostly joyful labor or drudgery? Explain. If you said drudgery, what are some ways you can rediscover the joy of ministry? Why is that important?

12. Paul was bold because of his confidence in what is unseen and eternal. How confident are you in the unseen things that made Paul confident? How does this affect the way you deal with hardship? With nonbelievers?

13. What compels you to do the things you do? In what ways does Christ's love compel you? In what ways do other things compel you? How can Christ's love be more and more the motivating force in your daily life?

Going Forward

14. Think of one or two things that you have learned that you'd like to work on in the coming week. Remember that this is all about quality, not quantity. It's better to work on one specific area of life and do it well than to work on many and do poorly (or to be so overwhelmed that you simply don't try).

Do you want to be more motivated by Christ's love? Be specific. Go back through 2 Corinthians 4—5 and put a star next to the phrase or verse that is most encouraging to you. Consider memorizing this verse.

Real-Life Application Ideas: Do a motive check on your ministry. Take stock of all the things you do in ministry—everything from simply attending church to leading worship or a small group or even sharing the good news with others. Examine your motive for each aspect of your ministry life. It might be helpful to have a close friend or pastor help you in this examination. If you find areas where your motives are anything other than God defined, consider what motives you would like to adopt. This might mean taking a break from some activities. It might mean changing your ministry focus. But it will certainly involve prayer, study, and seeking the wise counsel of others.

Seeking Help

15. Write a prayer below (or simply pray one in silence), inviting God to work on your mind and heart in those areas you've noted in the Going Forward section. Be honest about your desires and fears.

Notes for Small Groups:

- *Look for ways to put into practice the things you wrote in the Going Forward section. Talk with other group members about your ideas and commit to being accountable to one another.*

- *During the coming week, ask the Holy Spirit to continue to reveal truth to you from what you've read and studied.*

- *Before you start the next lesson, read 2 Corinthians 6—7. For more in-depth lesson preparation, read chapter 6, "Heart to Heart," in* Be Encouraged.

Heart to Heart
(2 CORINTHIANS 6—7)

Before you begin ...
- *Pray for the Holy Spirit to reveal truth and wisdom as you go through this lesson.*
- *Read 2 Corinthians 6—7. This lesson references chapter 6 in* Be Encouraged. *It will be helpful for you to have your Bible and a copy of the commentary available as you work through this lesson.*

Getting Started

From the Commentary

Second Corinthians 6 and 7 bring to a heartfelt conclusion Paul's explanation of his ministry. He has told his readers that, in spite of trials, his was a triumphant ministry (2 Cor. 1—2) and a glorious ministry (2 Cor. 3), and that he could not ever think of quitting. His enemies had accused him of using the ministry for personal gain, but he had proved his ministry to be sincere (2 Cor. 4) and based on faith in God (2 Cor. 5). All that remained now

was to challenge the hearts of the Corinthians and assure
them of his love.

—*Be Encouraged*, page 85

1. How did Paul prove his ministry was sincere? (See 2 Cor. 4.) How did
he prove it was based on faith in God? (See 2 Cor. 5.) Why did he spend
so many words defending his ministry? What are some of the ways pastors
and leaders today have to defend their ministries?

2. Choose one verse or phrase from 2 Corinthians 6—7 that stands out to
you. This could be something you're intrigued by, something that makes
you uncomfortable, something that puzzles you, something that resonates
with you, or just something you want to examine further. Write that here.

Going Deeper

From the Commentary

> *Principles of Psychology* by William James has been a classic text and certainly was a pioneer work in that field. But the author admitted that there was "an immense omission" in the book. "The deepest principle of human nature is the craving to be appreciated," he wrote; and yet he had not dealt with this principle in his book.
>
> As you read 2 Corinthians, you get the strong impression that the church did not really appreciate Paul and the work he had done among them. They should have been defending Paul and not forcing him to defend himself. The Corinthians were boasting about the Judaizers who had invaded the church, and yet the Judaizers had done nothing for them. So Paul reminded them of the ministry God had given him at Corinth.
>
> It was Paul who had gone to Corinth with the good news of the gospel; and through his ministry, the church had been founded. He had fulfilled the work of the "ambassador" described in 2 Corinthians 5:18–21. It was not the Judaizers who had won them to Christ; it was Paul.
>
> —*Be Encouraged*, pages 85–86

3. What are some examples from 2 Corinthians that reveal Paul's apparent belief that the Corinthians didn't appreciate him? Why did he choose to talk about his role as evangelist first when reminding them of his ministry

there? Does this suggest Paul was making the case that evangelism is the most important role in ministry? Explain.

More to Consider: In 2 Corinthians 6:2, why did Paul quote Isaiah 49:8 to the church? (See also 2 Cor. 13:5.) What was Paul's message to those who didn't yet know salvation? (See 2 Cor. 5:18–19; Isa. 55:6.)

From the Commentary

One of the greatest obstacles to the progress of the gospel is the bad example of people who profess to be Christians. Unsaved people like to use the inconsistencies of the saints—especially preachers—as an excuse for rejecting Jesus Christ. Paul was careful not to do anything that would put a stumbling block in the way of either sinners or saints (see Rom. 14). He did not want the ministry to be discredited ("blamed") in any way because of his life.

Paul reminded his readers of *the trials he had endured for them* (2 Cor. 6:4–5). He had been a man of endurance ("patience") and had not quit when things were tough.

Afflictions are trials under pressure, when you are pressed down by circumstances. *Necessities* are the everyday hardships of life, and *distresses* refer to experiences that push us into a corner where there seems to be no escape. The Greek word means "a narrow place."

—*Be Encouraged*, pages 86–87

4. Review 2 Corinthians 6:3–7. What were some of the trials and sacrifices Paul listed here? Why did he experience these trials? What big-picture message was Paul teaching through these verses?

From Today's World

Paul had a lot to say in defense of his ministry. Today's greatest church leaders often face the same sort of scrutiny Paul did. In a day where social media can pass along news faster than a fire in a windstorm, every misstep is immediate fodder for naysayers. There are plenty of examples in recent years where pastors have stated or even published something that might have caused followers to rethink their loyalties. A ministry leader's career can be questioned in an instant and even shattered by words that may or may not have been accurately represented.

5. How might Paul have used social media to make his case to the Corinthian church? What cautions would he have had about social media? What are ways he might have suggested it could be used for ministry? What are some of the challenges the modern church and its leaders face today in light of social media?

From the Commentary

> What a price Paul paid to be faithful in his ministry! And yet how little the Corinthians really appreciated all he did for them. They brought sorrow to his heart, yet he was "always rejoicing" in Jesus Christ. He became poor that they might become rich (see 1 Cor. 1:5; 2 Cor. 8:9). The word translated "poor" means "the complete destitution of a beggar."
>
> —*Be Encouraged*, pages 87–88

6. Was Paul wrong in appealing for the Corinthians' appreciation? Why or why not? Are today's pastors and leaders well appreciated for their ministry? Explain. What are some ways the modern church might do a better job appreciating its leaders?

From the Commentary

In spite of all the problems and heartaches the church had caused him, Paul still loved the believers at Corinth very much. He had spoken honestly and lovingly to them; now, in 2 Corinthians 6:11—7:1, he tenderly asked them to open their hearts to him. He felt like a father whose children were robbing him of the love that he deserved (see 1 Cor. 4:15).

Why were they withholding their love? Because they had divided hearts. The false teachers had stolen their hearts, and now they were cool toward Paul. They were like a daughter engaged to be married, but being seduced by an unworthy suitor (see 2 Cor. 11:1–3). The Corinthians were compromising with the world, so Paul appealed to them to separate themselves to God, the way a faithful wife is separated to her husband.

—*Be Encouraged*, page 88

7. How has the doctrine of separation to God been misunderstood in recent years? What is the difference between separation from the world and isolation from the world? What are some good ways to be separated? What are the risks of becoming isolated?

From the Commentary

Paul presented three arguments to try to convince these believers that they must separate themselves from that which is contrary to God's will.

The first argument is about the nature of the believer (2 Cor. 6:14–16). It is nature that determines association. Because a pig has a pig's nature, it associates with other pigs in the mud hole. Because a sheep has a sheep's nature, it munches grass with the flock in the pasture. The Christian possesses a divine nature (2 Peter 1:3–4).

—*Be Encouraged,* page 89

8. Read 2 Peter 1:3–4. What does it mean to have a "divine nature"? What does this nature reveal about Christians? About what they should want to associate themselves with?

More to Consider: Why did Paul use the plural when referring to "we are the temple" in 2 Corinthians 6:16? In what ways is the local church the dwelling place of God? (See Ex. 6:7; 25:8; Lev. 26:12; Ezek. 37:26–27.) What happens when a church compromises its testimony?

From the Commentary

Paul's second argument addresses the command of Scripture (2 Cor. 6:17). The major part of this quotation is from Isaiah 52:11, but there are also echoes in it of Ezekiel 20:34, 41. The reference in Isaiah is to the captive nation leaving Babylon and returning to their own land, but the spiritual application is to the separation of the people of God today.

And Paul's third argument focuses on the promise of God's blessing (2 Cor. 6:17—7:1). God becomes our Father when we trust Jesus Christ as our Savior, but He cannot *be to us* a Father unless we obey Him and fellowship with Him. He longs to receive us in love and treat us as His precious sons and daughters.

—*Be Encouraged*, pages 90–91

9. What are some ways in which separating ourselves from ungodly things can lead to God's blessing? If this separation is good for us and fits with our new nature, why do Christians so often find it hard to do?

From the Commentary

"Open wide your hearts to us!" (see 2 Cor. 6:13). "Receive us" (2 Cor. 7:2). "Can two walk together, except they be agreed?" (Amos 3:3). If the Corinthians would only cleanse their lives and their church fellowship, God would receive them (2 Cor. 6:17) and they could again have close fellowship with Paul.

The emphasis in 2 Corinthians 7:2–16 is on the way God encouraged Paul after he had experienced such great trials in Asia and Troas (see 2 Cor. 1:8–10; 2:12–13). There is actually a threefold encouragement recorded in these verses.

—Be Encouraged, page 93

10. Review 2 Corinthians 7:2–16. How did Paul encourage the church (vv. 2–4)? How did Titus encourage Paul (vv. 5–10)? How did the Corinthians encourage Titus (vv. 11–16)? What does this entire section reveal about the role of encouragement in ministry?

Looking Inward

Take a moment to reflect on all that you've explored thus far in this study of 2 Corinthians 6—7. Review your notes and answers and think about how each of these things matters in your life today.

> *Tips for Small Groups: To get the most out of this section, form pairs or trios and have group members take turns answering these questions. Be honest and as open as you can in this discussion, but most of all, be encouraging and supportive of others. Be sensitive to those who are going through particularly difficult times and don't press for people to speak if they're uncomfortable doing so.*

11. Have you endured trials and challenges in ministry that helped shape you? How have those times grown your faith? Improved your ability to minister? Do you ever feel like you aren't appreciated for all you've gone through? If so, what is a godly way to deal with that feeling?

12. What does it mean to you that you have a nature that has been shaped by your connection with God? How does that play out in everyday life? What are some aspects of your life where you have a hard time acting

according to this spiritual nature? What other nature is in conflict with this God-given nature?

13. How have you been encouraged in your ministry? How have you encouraged others? What are some practical ways you can encourage those who play leadership roles and support roles in your church? In what ways is encouragement itself a form of ministry?

Going Forward

14. Think of one or two things that you have learned that you'd like to work on in the coming week. Remember that this is all about quality, not quantity. It's better to work on one specific area of life and do it well than to work on many and do poorly (or to be so overwhelmed that you simply don't try).

Do you want to separate from something that isn't good for you? Be specific. Go back through 2 Corinthians 6—7 and put a star next to the phrase or verse that is most encouraging to you. Consider memorizing this verse.

Real-Life Application Ideas: Paul felt underappreciated in his role as minister. This week, work with other members of your church or small group to come up with plans for showing your leaders appreciation. This could be as simple as taking a pastor out to lunch or as involved as building an entire service around appreciation. Don't forget to include people who serve in less public roles too—worship director, choir director, accompanist, etc. Some of the ministry roles seem thankless at times. Use this opportunity to thank them in ways they won't soon forget.

Seeking Help

15. Write a prayer below (or simply pray one in silence), inviting God to work on your mind and heart in those areas you've noted in the Going Forward section. Be honest about your desires and fears.

Notes for Small Groups:

- *Look for ways to put into practice the things you wrote in the Going Forward section. Talk with other group members about your ideas and commit to being accountable to one another.*

- *During the coming week, ask the Holy Spirit to continue to reveal truth to you from what you've read and studied.*

- *Before you start the next lesson, read 2 Corinthians 8—9. For more in-depth lesson preparation, read chapters 7 and 8, "The Grace of Giving—Parts 1 and 2," in* Be Encouraged.

Giving
(2 CORINTHIANS 8—9)

Before you begin ...
- *Pray for the Holy Spirit to reveal truth and wisdom as you go through this lesson.*
- *Read 2 Corinthians 8—9. This lesson references chapters 7 and 8 in* Be Encouraged. *It will be helpful for you to have your Bible and a copy of the commentary available as you work through this lesson.*

Getting Started

From the Commentary

The Macedonian churches that Paul was using as an example had experienced severe difficulties, and yet they had given generously. They had not simply gone through "affliction"; they had experienced a "great trial of affliction" (2 Cor. 8:2). They were in *deep poverty*, which means "rock-bottom destitution." The word describes a beggar who has absolutely nothing and has no hope of getting anything. Their difficult situation may have been caused in part by their Christian faith, for they may have lost their jobs or been excluded from the trade guilds because they refused to have anything to do with idolatry.

When you have experienced the grace of God in your life, you will not use difficult circumstances as an excuse for not giving.

—*Be Encouraged*, pages 100–1

1. How can circumstances sometimes discourage giving? What did Paul teach about the real motive for giving? How does giving, according to the grace of God, transcend circumstances?

2. Choose one verse or phrase from 2 Corinthians 8—9 that stands out to you. This could be something you're intrigued by, something that makes you uncomfortable, something that puzzles you, something that resonates with you, or just something you want to examine further. Write that here.

Going Deeper

From the Commentary

> It is possible to give generously but not give enthusiastically. "The preacher says I should give until it hurts," said a miserly church member, "but for me, it hurts just to think about giving!" The Macedonian churches needed no prompting or reminding, as did the church at Corinth. They were more than willing to share in the collection. In fact, *they begged to be included* (2 Cor. 8:4 NASB)! How many times have you heard a Christian *beg* for somebody to take an offering?
>
> —*Be Encouraged*, page 101

3. Review 2 Corinthians 8:3–4. The Macedonians gave voluntarily. What does this say about their motives for giving? In what ways was their giving an act of celebration? How does this compare to the Corinthians? How does it compare with the way giving is treated in the modern church?

More to Consider: Read the following verses: Deuteronomy 15:10; 16:17; 1 Chronicles 29:9; Proverbs 3:9–10, 27; 11:24–25; 21:26; 22:9. How does each passage add to Paul's message about giving?

From the Commentary

Jesus Christ is always the preeminent example for the believer to follow, whether in service, suffering, or sacrifice. Like Jesus Christ, the Macedonian Christians *gave themselves to God and to others* (2 Cor. 8:5). If we give ourselves to God, we will have little problem giving our substance to God. If we give ourselves to God, we will also give of ourselves for others. It is impossible to love God and ignore the needs of your neighbor. Jesus Christ gave Himself for us (Gal. 1:4; 2:20). Should we not give ourselves to Him? He died so that we might not live for ourselves, but for Him and for others (2 Cor. 5:15).

The Macedonians' giving was, like Christ's, *motivated by love* (2 Cor. 8:7–8). What a rebuke to the Corinthians, who were so enriched with spiritual blessings (1 Cor. 1:4–5). They were so wrapped up in the *gifts* of the Spirit that they had neglected the *graces* of the Spirit, including the grace of giving. The Macedonian churches had an "abundance of ... deep poverty" (2 Cor. 8:2), and yet they abounded in their liberality. The Corinthians had an abundance of spiritual gifts, yet they were lax in keeping their promise and sharing in the collection.

—*Be Encouraged*, page 102

4. Review 2 Corinthians 8:5–9. Why is an abundance of spiritual gifts not a substitute for generous giving? How do people in church today use a similar argument to explain their giving habits (or lack thereof)? Why is giving important not just for the few who have a lot but for all Christians?

From the Commentary

There is a great difference between *promise* and *performance*. The Corinthians had boasted to Titus a year before that they would share in the special collection (2 Cor. 8:6), but they did not keep their promise. Note that in 2 Corinthians 8:10–12 Paul emphasized *willingness*. Grace giving must come from a willing heart; it cannot be coerced or forced.

During my years of ministry, I have endured many offering appeals. I have listened to pathetic tales about unbelievable needs. I have forced myself to laugh at old jokes that were supposed to make it easier for me to part with my money. I have been scolded, shamed, and almost threatened, and I must confess that none of these approaches has ever stirred me to give more than I planned to give. In fact, more than once I gave *less* because I was so disgusted with the worldly approach. (However, I have never gotten like Mark Twain, who said that he was so sickened by the long appeal that he not only did not give what he planned to give, but he also took a bill out of the plate!)

We must be careful here not to confuse *willing* with *doing*, because the two must go together. If the willing is sincere and in the will of God, then there must be "a performance also" (2 Cor. 8:11; see Phil. 2:12–13). Paul did not say that *willing* was a substitute for *doing*, because it is not. But if our giving is motivated by grace, we will give willingly, and not because we have been forced to give.

—*Be Encouraged*, page 104

5. What's the key difference between being willing to give and actually giving? How do our actions reveal the willingness in our hearts? (See Phil. 2:12–13.) What do today's pledge drives and other appeals for money reveal about our willingness? Is there a better way to approach this subject in the local church? Explain.

From the Commentary

Paul did not suggest that the rich become poor so that the poor might become rich. It would be unwise for a Christian to go into debt in order to relieve somebody else's debt, unless, of course, he was able to handle the responsibility of paying the debt back. Paul saw an "equality" in the whole procedure: the Gentiles were enriched spiritually by the Jews, so the Jews should be enriched materially by the Gentiles (see Rom. 15:25–28). Furthermore, the Gentile churches at that time were enjoying some measure of material wealth, while the believers in Judea were suffering. That situation could one day be reversed. There might come a time when the Jewish believers would be assisting the Gentiles.

—*Be Encouraged*, page 105

6. Review 2 Corinthians 8:13–24. What was the equality Paul saw in his examination of giving? Who does the equalizing? What example did Paul give to support this? (See Ex. 16:18.)

From the Commentary

While Christians must not compete with each other in their service for Christ, they ought to "consider one another to provoke unto love and to good works" (Heb. 10:24). When we see what God is doing in and through the lives of others, we ought to strive to serve Him better ourselves. There is a fine line between fleshly imitation and spiritual emulation, and we must be careful in this regard. But a zealous Christian can be the means of stirring up a church and motivating people to pray, work, witness, and give.

The interesting thing is this: Paul had used the zeal of the Corinthians to challenge the Macedonians; but now he was using the Macedonians to challenge the Corinthians! A year before, the Corinthians had enthusiastically boasted that they would share in the offering, but then they had done nothing. The Macedonians had followed through on their promise, and Paul was afraid that his boasting would be in vain.

—*Be Encouraged*, pages 113–14

7. How did Paul make the argument that it's okay to be "provoked unto love"? What did this look like in Paul's day? Does the modern church provoke people to love? Explain.

From the Commentary

"Give, and it shall be given unto you," was our Lord's promise; and it still holds true (Luke 6:38). The "good measure" He gives back to us is not always money or material goods, but it is always worth far more than we gave. Giving is not something we *do*, but something we *are*. Giving is a way of life for the Christian who understands the grace of God. The world simply does not understand a statement like Proverbs 11:24 (NIV): "One man gives freely, yet gains even more; another withholds unduly, but comes to poverty." In grace giving, our motive is not "to get something," but receiving God's blessing is one of the fringe benefits.

—Be Encouraged, page 115

8. What principles of giving did Paul present in 2 Corinthians 9:6–11? How do these principles make giving a blessing? Why is this a difficult concept to understand in today's world?

More to Consider: The word sufficiency *means "adequate resources within" (see Phil. 4:11). How does Jesus Christ provide us with the adequacy to meet the demands of life? (See John 4:14.)*

From the Commentary

Paul introduced a new word for the offering: *service*. It means "priestly service," so once again, Paul lifted the offering to the highest level possible. He saw this collection as a "spiritual sacrifice" presented to God, the way a priest presented a costly sacrifice on the altar.

Christians no longer bring animals as sacrifices to God, because the work of Christ on the cross has ended the Levitical system (Heb. 10:1–14). But the material gifts we bring to the Lord become "spiritual sacrifices" if they are given in the name of Jesus (Phil. 4:10–20; Heb. 13:15–16; 1 Peter 2:5).

But the emphasis in 2 Corinthians 9:12 is on the fact that their offering would meet the needs of poor saints in Judea. "For the administration of this service not only supplieth the want of the saints, but is abundant also by many thanksgivings unto God" (2 Cor. 9:12). The Gentile believers could have given a number of excuses for not giving. "It's not our fault that they had a famine and are poor!" might have been one of them. Or, "The churches closer to Judea ought to give them help." Or, "We believe in giving, but we think we should first take care of our own."

—*Be Encouraged*, page 119

9. What are some of the excuses believers give today for not giving to a cause? What do these reasons reveal about their hearts? How do we know when it's right to give and when it's best to use the money or offering in another way?

From the Commentary

"Let your light so shine before men," said our Lord, "that they may see your good works, and glorify your Father which is in heaven" (Matt. 5:16). This is one of the beauties of church giving: no individual gets the glory that belongs only to God.

For what would the grateful Jewish believers give thanks? Of course, they would praise God for the generosity of the Gentile churches in meeting their physical and material needs. But they would also praise God for the spiritual submission of the Gentiles, their obedience to the Spirit of God who gave them the desire to give. They would say, "Those Gentiles not only preach the gospel, but they also practice it!"

—*Be Encouraged*, pages 120–21

10. Review 2 Corinthians 9:13. What is the significance of the little phrase "and unto all men" (KJV; "and with everyone else" NIV) at the end of this verse? How does this reveal the importance of giving by grace and not out of guilt or coercion?

Looking Inward

Take a moment to reflect on all that you've explored thus far in this study of 2 Corinthians 8—9. Review your notes and answers and think about how each of these things matters in your life today.

> *Tips for Small Groups: To get the most out of this section, form pairs or trios and have group members take turns answering these questions. Be honest and as open as you can in this discussion, but most of all, be encouraging and supportive of others. Be sensitive to those who are going through particularly difficult times and don't press for people to speak if they're uncomfortable doing so.*

11. When have you given despite hardship? How easy or difficult was that for you? Why did you give anyway? Describe a time when you didn't give because you were suffering hardship. Did you feel guilty about this? If so, how did you resolve that guilt?

12. Have you ever told yourself "But I do this [specific act] for the church, so I don't have to give [time, money, etc.]"? Explain. Why did you try to make the case that you didn't need to give beyond what you already offered? What might Paul say to you about this attitude?

13. Describe a time when you felt coerced into giving. What led to that situation? How did you respond? Can you find a way to give out of grace, even when the invitation to give feels more like a demand? Explain.

Going Forward

14. Think of one or two things that you have learned that you'd like to work on in the coming week. Remember that this is all about quality, not quantity. It's better to work on one specific area of life and do it well than to work on many and do poorly (or to be so overwhelmed that you simply don't try).

Do you want to learn how to give out of grace? Be specific. Go back through 2 Corinthians 8—9 and put a star next to the phrase or verse that is most encouraging to you. Consider memorizing this verse.

Real-Life Application Ideas: Consider your giving habits. This doesn't mean only your money but also your time. Look at the various ways you give to those in need, whether through the ministry of the church or other ministries. Do you feel as if you're giving out of grace? If so, thank God for giving you a grace-filled heart. If not, ask God to help you let go of selfish desires so you can give without complaint. Then look for practical ways to act on this kind of giving.

Seeking Help

15. Write a prayer below (or simply pray one in silence), inviting God to work on your mind and heart in those areas you've noted in the Going Forward section. Be honest about your desires and fears.

Notes for Small Groups:

- *Look for ways to put into practice the things you wrote in the Going Forward section. Talk with other group members about your ideas and commit to being accountable to one another.*

- *During the coming week, ask the Holy Spirit to continue to reveal truth to you from what you've read and studied.*

- *Before you start the next lesson, read 2 Corinthians 10. For more in-depth lesson preparation, read chapter 9, "Ministerial Misunderstandings," in* Be Encouraged.

Misunderstandings
(2 CORINTHIANS 10)

Before you begin ...
- *Pray for the Holy Spirit to reveal truth and wisdom as you go through this lesson.*
- *Read 2 Corinthians 10. This lesson references chapter 9 in* Be Encouraged. *It will be helpful for you to have your Bible and a copy of the commentary available as you work through this lesson.*

Getting Started

From the Commentary

Whenever I receive a critical letter from a reader or a radio listener, I usually set it aside in a special file until I feel I am really ready to answer it. On a few occasions, I have replied to letters too quickly, and I have regretted it. By waiting, I give myself time to think and pray, to read between the lines, and to prepare a reply that would do the most good and the least damage.

The Spirit led Paul to use a wise approach as he wrote to the Corinthians. He was writing to a divided church (1 Cor. 1:11ff.), a church that was resisting his authority, and a church that was being seduced by false teachers. So, first he explained his ministry so that they would no longer doubt his sincerity. He then encouraged them to share in the offering, for he knew that this challenge would help them grow in their spiritual lives. Grace giving and grace living go together.

Now, in the last section of the letter, Paul challenged the rebels in the church—including the false teachers—and enforced his apostolic ministry.

Paul was not involved in a "personality contest" with other ministers. His enemies did not hesitate to accuse him falsely, nor did they hesitate to promote themselves (2 Cor. 11:12). It was the worldly attitude of the Corinthians that *forced* Paul to defend himself by reminding them of his life and ministry. Paul never hesitated to talk about Jesus Christ, but he did refuse to talk about himself, unless there was good reason to do so.

—*Be Encouraged*, pages 127–28

1. How did Paul defend his apostolic authority in this passage? How is this different from a personal defense? Why is this important?

More to Consider: Paul used the word translated "boast" or "glory" twenty times in 2 Corinthians 10—13. (Circle these in your Bible.) Now read Romans 5:11; Galatians 6:14; Philippians 3:3; 2 Corinthians 7:4, 14; 8:24. What do these passages reveal about the reason for these words? How did Paul glory in Jesus Christ and not in himself?

2. Choose one verse or phrase from 2 Corinthians 10 that stands out to you. This could be something you're intrigued by, something that makes you uncomfortable, something that puzzles you, something that resonates with you, or just something you want to examine further. Write that here.

Going Deeper

From the Commentary

The rebels in the church (led by the Judaizers) said that Paul was very courageous when he wrote letters from a distance, but very timid and even weak when he was present with the Corinthians (see also 2 Cor. 10:9–11). The Judaizers, of course, were consistently overbearing in their attitudes—and the people loved them (2 Cor. 11:20). Paul's "inconsistent" manner of life paralleled his "yes and no" approach to making promises (2 Cor. 1:15–20).

When Paul founded the church at Corinth, his purpose was to exalt Christ and not himself (1 Cor. 2:1–5). Christians usually grow the way they are born. If they are born in an atmosphere of dictatorial leadership, they grow up depending on man's wisdom and strength. If they are born in an atmosphere of humility and love, they learn to depend on the Lord. Paul wanted his converts to trust the Lord, and not the servant; so he deliberately "played down" his own authority and ability.

—*Be Encouraged*, pages 128–29

3. Review 2 Corinthians 10:1–2. How did Paul's attitude in these verses disarm his opponents? What did the Corinthians fail to realize about the real source of spiritual power?

From the Commentary

The word *warfare* in 2 Corinthians 10:4 means "campaign." Paul was not simply fighting a little skirmish in

Corinth; the attack of the enemy there was part of a large satanic campaign. The powers of hell are still trying to destroy the work of God (Matt. 16:18), and it is important that we not yield any ground to the enemy, not even one church!

There are walls of resistance in the minds of people, and these walls (like the walls of Jericho) must be pulled down. What are these "mental walls"? Reasonings that are opposed to the truth of God's Word. Pride of intelligence that exalts itself. Paul had faced this "wisdom of men" when he founded the church (1 Cor. 1:18ff.), and it had surfaced again with the coming of the Judaizers.

Paul's attitude of humility was actually one of his strongest weapons, for pride plays right into the hands of Satan. The meek Son of God had far more power than Pilate (see John 19:11), and He proved it. Paul used spiritual weapons to tear down the opposition—prayer, the Word of God, love, the power of the Spirit at work in his life. He did not depend on personality, human abilities, or even the authority he had as an apostle. However, he was ready to punish the offenders, if necessary, once the congregation had submitted to the Lord.

—*Be Encouraged*, page 130

4. Respond to the following statement: Paul was not attacking intelligence, but intellectualism. (See Rom. 12:16.) Why was it necessary to attack intellectualism? What are the dangers of intellectualism?

From Today's World

Paul's battle was primarily with the Judaizers in the Corinthian church, but modern churches often fight battles on multiple fronts. Not only are there internal skirmishes between factions arguing over a particular point of view, theology, or where to put the piano, but there are also external battles. The external battles aren't just for souls—they're also battles with media and the court of public opinion. Every mistake or poor choice made by someone in a position of leadership in a church is broadly applied to all of Christianity by many nonbelievers. A person in the public eye is presumed to represent the whole of the church, and this creates a real challenge for local churches trying to make their congregations a welcoming, warm place for nonbelievers.

5. How important is the public image of the church? What are some of the unique challenges the church faces today with regard to how the world views it? Can the local church win these battles? Why or why not?

From the Commentary

One of the most difficult lessons Christ's disciples had to learn was that, in the kingdom of God, position and power were no evidence of authority. Jesus warned His followers not to pattern their leadership after that of the Gentiles who loved to "lord it over" others and to act important (see Mark 10:35–45). The example we must follow is that of Jesus Christ, who came as a servant and ministered to others. Paul followed that example.

But the Corinthians were not spiritually minded enough to discern what Paul was doing. They contrasted his meekness with the "personality power" of the Judaizers, and they concluded that Paul had no authority at all. To be sure, he wrote powerful letters; but his physical appearance was weak, and his speech "unimpressive." They were judging by the outward appearance and were not exercising spiritual discernment.

—*Be Encouraged*, page 131

6. Review 2 Corinthians 10:7–11. How were position and power abused in the Corinthian church? How does this happen today? Why are we quick to judge based on outward appearances? How can we learn to exercise spiritual discernment?

From the Commentary

> The opponents in the church were accusing Paul of not
> being a true apostle; for, if he were a true apostle, he would
> show it by using his authority. On the other hand, if Paul
> *had* thrown his weight around, they would have found
> fault with that. No matter what course Paul took, they
> were bound to condemn him. This is what always hap-
> pens when church members are not spiritually minded,
> but evaluate ministry from a worldly viewpoint.
>
> But their accusation backfired. If Paul was not an apostle,
> then he was a counterfeit and not even a believer. But
> if that were true, then the church at Corinth was not a
> true church. Paul had already made it clear that nobody
> could separate his ministry and his personal life (2 Cor.
> 1:12–14).
>
> —*Be Encouraged*, page 132

7. How did the accusations of Paul's opponents backfire? How did Paul's
assertion that his personal life and ministry couldn't be separated answer
their accusations? (See 2 Cor. 1:12–14.) Respond to this statement: If Paul
were a deceiver, then the Corinthians were the deceived.

From the Commentary

How a Christian uses authority is an evidence of his spiritual maturity and character. An immature person *swells* as he uses his authority, but a mature person *grows* in the use of authority, and others grow with him. The wise pastor, like the wise parent, knows when to wait in loving patience and when to act with determined power. It takes more power to wait than to strike. A mature person does not use authority to *demand* respect, but to *command* respect. Mature leaders suffer while they wait to act, while immature leaders act impetuously and make others suffer.

The false teachers depended on "letters of recommendation" for their authority, but Paul had a divine commission from heaven. The life that he lived and the work that he did were "credentials" enough, for it was evident that the hand of God was on his life.

—*Be Encouraged*, page 133

8. How is the Corinthian problem an example of the adage "Power corrupts"? What were Paul's credentials? (See Gal. 6:17.) Why did the Corinthians have a hard time accepting these?

From the Commentary

I suppose more problems have been caused by people "measuring the ministry" than by any other activity in the church. If the work of the church is the work of God, and if the work of God is a miracle, how do we go about measuring a miracle? In His personal examination of the seven churches named in Revelation 2 and 3, the Lord Jesus measured them far differently than they measured themselves. The church that thought it was poor, He considered to be rich; and the church that boasted of its wealth, He declared to be poor (Rev. 2:8–11; 3:14–22).

Some people measure ministry only by statistics. While it is true that the early church did take note of numbers (Acts 2:41; 4:4), it is also true that uniting with the church at that time was a much more difficult (and dangerous) thing (see Acts 5:13). Some years ago, one of America's large denominations had as its theme, "A Million More in '64, and Every One a Tither!" I heard one of their leading preachers comment, "If we get a million more like the last million, God help us!" Quantity is no guarantee of quality.

—*Be Encouraged*, page 134

9. Review 2 Corinthians 10:12–18. How did the Corinthian church measure ministry? How do modern churches measure it? Why are we so obsessed with numbers and statistics? What should we be concerned with in the church? How can we balance the relative value of numbers with the infinite value of souls?

More to Consider: In a sense, the Judaizers belonged to a "mutual admiration society" that set up its own standards and measured everybody by them. Of course, those inside the group were successful; those outside were failures. Read Ephesians 4:12–16. How would using the measure described in this passage have drastically changed the situation?

From the Commentary

Churches and ministers are not competing with each other; they are competing with themselves. God is not going to measure us on the basis of the gifts and opportunities that He gave to Charles Spurgeon or Billy Sunday. He will measure my work by what He assigned to me. God requires faithfulness above everything else (1 Cor. 4:2).

There is something intimidating about attending a pastors' conference or a denominational convention, because the people on the program are usually the "front-runners" with the best records. Young pastors and older men in narrow places often go home carrying feelings of guilt because their faithful work does not seem to produce as much fruit. Some of these discouraged men then try all kinds of programs and promotions, only to have more disappointment; and then they contemplate leaving the ministry. If only they would realize that God measures their ministries on the basis of where He has put them, and not on the basis of what is going on in some other city, it would encourage them to stay on the job and keep being faithful.

—*Be Encouraged,* page 135

10. Why did Paul quote Jeremiah 9:24 in 2 Corinthians 10:17? What's the problem with competition among church leaders? Why was this damaging the Corinthian church? How does it damage our churches today?

Looking Inward

Take a moment to reflect on all that you've explored thus far in this study of 2 Corinthians 10. Review your notes and answers and think about how each of these things matters in your life today.

Tips for Small Groups: To get the most out of this section, form pairs or trios and have group members take turns answering these questions. Be honest and as open as you can in this discussion, but most of all, be encouraging and supportive of others. Be sensitive to those who are going through particularly difficult times and don't press for people to speak if they're uncomfortable doing so.

11. How skilled are you at spiritual discernment? How do you know when you're in God's will and when you're fighting against it? What is the role of spiritual discernment in your daily life?

12. What are some ways you measure ministry in your church? How can your spiritual discernment help you overcome the temptation to judge ministry by numbers and other worldly measures?

13. Have you ever competed with other church members (whether they knew it or not) in matters of ministry? What prompted this? How did it turn out? Where was God in the midst of the desire to "win" against a fellow believer?

Going Forward

14. Think of one or two things that you have learned that you'd like to work on in the coming week. Remember that this is all about quality, not quantity. It's better to work on one specific area of life and do it well than to work on many and do poorly (or to be so overwhelmed that you simply don't try).

Do you want to learn discernment? Be specific. Go back through 2 Corinthians 10 and put a star next to the phrase or verse that is most encouraging to you. Consider memorizing this verse.

Real-Life Application Ideas: Consider how your church measures its ministry. Are you more of a "fill the pews" church, or a church dedicated to the individual, no matter how many show up on Sunday? How would you change the way your church measures the success of its ministry? Talk with a senior pastor about your ideas, and work together to be a church that focuses first on ministering to the individual.

Seeking Help

15. Write a prayer below (or simply pray one in silence), inviting God to work on your mind and heart in those areas you've noted in the Going Forward section. Be honest about your desires and fears.

Notes for Small Groups:

- *Look for ways to put into practice the things you wrote in the Going Forward section. Talk with other group members about your ideas and commit to being accountable to one another.*
- *During the coming week, ask the Holy Spirit to continue to reveal truth to you from what you've read and studied.*
- *Before you start the next lesson, read 2 Corinthians 11:1—12:10. For more in-depth lesson preparation, read chapters 10 and 11, "Father Knows Best" and "A Preacher in Paradise," in* Be Encouraged.

Ministry and Defense
(2 CORINTHIANS 11:1—12:10)

Before you begin …
- *Pray for the Holy Spirit to reveal truth and wisdom as you go through this lesson.*
- *Read 2 Corinthians 11:1—12:10. This lesson references chapters 10 and 11 in* Be Encouraged. *It will be helpful for you to have your Bible and a copy of the commentary available as you work through this lesson.*

Getting Started

From the Commentary

True love is never envious, but it has a right to be jealous over those who are loved. A husband is jealous over his wife and rightfully resents and resists any rivalry that threatens their love for each other. A true patriot has every right to be jealous over his freedom and will fight to protect it. Likewise, a father (or a mother) is jealous over his or her children and seeks to protect them from anything that will harm them.

The *picture* here is that of a loving father who has a daughter engaged to be married. He feels it is his privilege and duty to keep her pure, so that he can present her to her husband with joy and not with sorrow. Paul saw the local church as a bride, engaged to be married to Jesus Christ (see Eph. 5:22ff.; Rom. 7:4). That marriage will not take place until Jesus Christ has come for His bride (Rev. 19:1–9). Meanwhile, the church—and this means individual Christians—must keep herself pure as she prepares to meet her Beloved.

—*Be Encouraged*, pages 141–42

1. Review 2 Corinthians 11:1–6, 13–15. In light of Paul's other teachings on marriage, why do you think he chose the marriage metaphor for the church? What does it mean that the church must keep "pure" in preparation for the wedding? How did Paul counsel the Corinthians in this matter?

More to Consider: Read Jeremiah 2:2 and Revelation 2:4. What does the frequent use of marriage imagery in the Bible reveal about God? About His love for His people? What does it mean to treat God as our "first love"?

2. Choose one verse or phrase from 2 Corinthians 11:1—12:10 that stands out to you. This could be something you're intrigued by, something that makes you uncomfortable, something that puzzles you, something that resonates with you, or just something you want to examine further. Write that here.

Going Deeper

From the Commentary

> The *person behind the peril* was Satan, pictured here as the serpent. The reference is to Genesis 3.
>
> The focus here is on the mind, for Satan is a liar and tries to get us to listen to his lies, ponder them, and then believe them. This is what he did with Eve. First, he *questioned* God's word ("Yea, hath God said?"), then he *denied* God's

word ("Ye shall not surely die"), and then he *substituted his own lie* ("Ye shall be as gods") (see Gen. 3:1, 4–5).

Satan, of course, is crafty. He knows that believers will not immediately accept a lie, so the enemy has to "bait the hook" and make it easy for us to accept what he has to offer. Basically, Satan is an imitator: he copies what God does and then tries to convince us that his offer is better than God's. How does he do this? By using counterfeit ministers who pretend to serve God, but who are really the servants of Satan.

Satan has a counterfeit gospel (Gal. 1:6–12) that involves a different savior and a different spirit.

Paul proved his love for the church by protecting it from the attacks of false teachers; and yet the members of the church "fell for" the Judaizers and let them come in. The Corinthians had "left their first love" and were no longer giving single-hearted devotion to Jesus Christ. It was not only that they had turned against Paul, but they had turned away from Christ; and that was far more serious.

—*Be Encouraged*, pages 142–44

3. Why is it notable that Paul said so much about our adversary, the Devil, in this letter to the Corinthians? What warnings did Paul offer? (See 2 Cor. 2:10–11; 4:4; 11:3; 12:7.) How do these warnings apply to the church today?

From the Commentary

A loving parent provides for the needs of the family, and Paul sacrificed that he might minister to the church at Corinth. While Paul was there, he labored with his own hands as a tentmaker (Acts 18:1–3) and even received gifts from other churches so that he might evangelize Corinth. In other words, it had cost the Corinthians nothing to benefit from the apostolic ministry of this great man of God.

Did the Corinthians appreciate the sacrifices that Paul made for them? No, most of them did not. In fact, the Judaizers even used Paul's financial policy as "proof" that he was not a true apostle. After all, if he *were* a true apostle, he would accept financial support.

Paul had already explained his policy in a previous letter (1 Cor. 9). He had pointed out that he *was* a true apostle because he had seen the risen Christ and had been commissioned by Him. Paul had the right to ask for financial support, just as God's faithful servants do today; but he had deliberately given up that right so that nobody could accuse him of using the gospel simply as a means of making money. He gave up his "financial rights" for the gospel's sake and for the sake of lost sinners who might stumble over anything that gave the impression of being "religious business."

—*Be Encouraged*, pages 144–45

4. Review 2 Corinthians 11:7–12. Why wouldn't Paul accept financial support just to appease the naysayers? What does this say about Paul? What lesson does this give to leaders today?

From the Commentary

The key to 2 Corinthians 11:16–33 is verse 28, which could be paraphrased: "Yes, I have been through many trials, but the greatest trial of all, the heaviest burden of all, is my concern for the churches!" The word translated "care" means "pressure, stress, anxiety." The other experiences were external ("without") and occasional, but the burden of the churches was internal and constant.

"We never know the love of our parents for us till we have become parents," said Henry Ward Beecher, and he was right. When our older son was a tot, he pushed a toy into the electrical outlet and was "zapped" across the room. (We didn't have the word *zap* in those days, but that's still what happened.) One day recently he discovered his own little son playing with the outlet, and his explosive response nearly frightened the child out of a year's growth. "Now I know how you and Mom felt when I was a kid," he told me over the phone. "Being a parent has its fears as well as its joys."

—*Be Encouraged*, page 147

5. Why did Paul feel the need to explain why he was boasting in this way? In his attempts to avoid lifting himself up, Paul might seem to have been accomplishing the opposite. What's the line between self-promotion and God-promotion? How did Paul walk that line in this letter?

From the Commentary

When it came to their Jewish heritage, the false teachers were equal to Paul; but when it came to ministry for Christ, it was Paul who was the "super-apostle" and not the Judaizers. Consider what Paul endured for the cause of Christ and the care of the churches.

Had Paul not been an apostle, he would not have experienced these trials. He received "stripes above measure" from both the Gentiles and from the Jews. Three times the Gentiles beat him with rods, and five times he was given thirty-nine lashes by the Jews. Only one beating is recorded in the book of Acts (16:22), as well as the one stoning (Acts 14:19).

Paul knew from the outset of his ministry that he would suffer for Jesus' sake (Acts 9:15–16), and God reaffirmed this to him as his ministry continued (Acts 20:23). He who caused others to suffer for their faith, himself had to suffer for his faith.

Almost any traveler in that day could have experienced some of these hardships; yet we cannot help but believe that they were caused by the enemy in an attempt to hinder the work of the Lord. Acts 27 records one of the three shipwrecks; we know nothing about the other two. We wonder how many of his precious personal possessions Paul lost in this way.

—*Be Encouraged*, page 149

6. Paul's need to constantly defend his apostleship can appear self-centered at times. If we assume his defense was warranted, what does this say about the kinds of attacks he endured? What are similar stories in the church today? At what point does defending a ministry become more about the person than the ministry?

From the Commentary

The Judaizers were anxious to receive honors, and they boasted about their "letters of commendation" (2 Cor. 3:1ff.). But Paul did not look for honor from men; he let God honor him, for that alone is the honor that really counts.

First, God honored Paul by giving him visions and revelations. Paul saw the glorified Christ on the very day he was converted (Acts 9:3ff.; 22:6). He saw a vision of Ananias coming to minister to him (Acts 9:12), and he also had a vision from God when he was called to minister to the Gentiles (Acts 22:17ff.).

During his ministry, he had visions from God to guide him and encourage him. It was by a vision that he was called to Macedonia (Acts 16:9). When the ministry was difficult in Corinth, God encouraged Paul by a vision (Acts 18:9–10). After his arrest in Jerusalem, Paul was again encouraged by a vision from God (Acts 23:11). An angel appeared to him in the midst of the storm and assured him that he and the passengers would be saved (Acts 27:23).

—*Be Encouraged,* pages 153–54

7. Review 2 Corinthians 12:1–6. Why did the Judaizers covet honor and accolades from men? How did they go about this? What happens when people in leadership pursue acknowledgment from man rather than God? What are some examples of this in today's church?

From the Commentary

The Lord knows how to balance our lives. If we have only blessings, we may become proud; so He permits us to have burdens as well. Paul's great experience in heaven could have ruined his ministry on earth; so God, in His goodness, permitted Satan to buffet Paul in order to keep him from becoming proud.

The mystery of human suffering will not be solved completely in this life. Sometimes we suffer simply because we are human. Our bodies change as we grow older, and we are susceptible to the normal problems of life. The same body that can bring us pleasures can also bring us pains. The same family members and friends who delight us can also break our hearts. This is a part of the "human comedy," and the only way to escape it is to be less than human. But nobody wants to take that route.

Sometimes we suffer because we are foolish and disobedient to the Lord. Our own rebellion may afflict us, or the Lord may see fit to chasten us in His love (Heb. 12:3ff.). King David suffered greatly because of his sin; the consequences were painful and so was the discipline of God (see 2 Sam. 12:1–22; Ps. 51). In His grace, God forgives our sins; but in His government, He must permit us to reap what we sow.

Suffering also is a tool God uses for building godly character (Rom. 5:1–5). Certainly Paul was a man of rich

Christian character because he permitted God to mold and make him in the painful experiences of his life.

—*Be Encouraged*, page 156

8. How does God use suffering to build godly character? (See Rom. 5:1–5.) How did He do this with Paul? How does He do this with us today?

More to Consider: Read Job 1—2. How is Paul's circumstance similar to Job's? How can God's power to control evil be used for His own glory?

From the Commentary

The thorn in the flesh was Satan's message to Paul, but God had another message for him, a message of grace. The tense of the verb in 2 Corinthians 12:9 is important: "And he said unto me." God gave Paul a message that stayed with him. The words Paul heard while in heaven, he was not permitted to share with us; but he did share the words God gave him on earth—and what an encouragement they are.

It was a message of grace. What is grace? It is God's provision for our every need when we need it. It has well been said that God in His grace gives us what we do not deserve, and in His mercy He does not give us what we do deserve. Someone has made an acrostic of the word grace: God's Riches Available at Christ's Expense. "And of his [Christ's] fullness have all we received, and grace for grace" (John 1:16).

—*Be Encouraged*, page 159

9. Review 2 Corinthians 12:9–10. How is this a message of "sufficient" grace? (See also 2 Cor. 3:4–6; 9:8; 12:9). How does knowing God's grace is sufficient help us in times of suffering? How does it help us when times are good? Why was sufficiency such an important message for the Corinthians? Why is it important for us today?

From the Commentary

What benefits did Paul receive because of his suffering? For one thing, he experienced the power of Christ in his life. God transformed Paul's weakness into strength. The word translated "rest" means "to spread a tent over." Paul saw his body as a frail tent (2 Cor. 5:1ff.), but the glory of God had come into that tent and transformed it into a holy tabernacle.

Something else happened to Paul: he was able to glory in his infirmities. This does not mean that he preferred pain to health, but rather that he knew how to turn his infirmities into assets. What made the difference? The grace of God *and* the glory of God. He "took pleasure" in these trials and problems, not because he was psychologically unbalanced and enjoyed pain, but because he was suffering for the sake of Jesus Christ. He was glorifying God by the way he accepted and handled the difficult experiences of life.

"It is a greater thing to pray for pain's conversion than for its removal," wrote P. T. Forsyth, and this is true. Paul won the victory, not by substitution, but by transformation. He discovered the sufficiency of the grace of God.

—*Be Encouraged*, page 161

10. What practical lessons can we learn from Paul's suffering? How does the statement by P. T. Forsyth in the previous excerpt from *Be Encouraged* ring true for Paul? How can we live this truth out in practical ways today?

Looking Inward

Take a moment to reflect on all that you've explored thus far in this study of 2 Corinthians 11:1—12:10. Review your notes and answers and think about how each of these things matters in your life today.

> *Tips for Small Groups: To get the most out of this section, form pairs or trios and have group members take turns answering these questions. Be honest and as open as you can in this discussion, but most of all, be encouraging and supportive of others. Be sensitive to those who are going through particularly difficult times and don't press for people to speak if they're uncomfortable doing so.*

11. Do you ever make decisions just to appease others, even when those decisions might go against what God would have you do? Explain. What does this say about your understanding of God's will? Your trust level in matters of faith?

12. Describe a time when you were tempted to pursue acknowledgment from people rather than from God. Why do you long for the acceptance of other people? When this is in conflict with what God wants, where do you turn to find the strength to pursue God's "well done" rather than people's?

13. Paul welcomed suffering as an opportunity to grow in faith. How have you grown from pain—whether physical or emotional or psychological? Was this an easy lesson to learn? Why or why not?

Going Forward

14. Think of one or two things that you have learned that you'd like to work on in the coming week. Remember that this is all about quality, not quantity. It's better to work on one specific area of life and do it well than to work on many and do poorly (or to be so overwhelmed that you simply don't try).

Do you want to pursue spiritual growth in the midst of pain? Be specific. Go back through 2 Corinthians 11:1—12:10 and put a star next to the phrase or verse that is most encouraging to you. Consider memorizing this verse.

Real-Life Application Ideas: Practice what Paul preached (and lived out) by doing some things for God alone this week. Don't seek out the affirmation of other people for your actions—don't tell anyone at all about what you are doing. Just take action to bring glory to God (sharing the good news, doing acts of service, fasting and praying, etc.), and let the knowledge that God smiles upon you be enough.

Seeking Help

15. Write a prayer below (or simply pray one in silence), inviting God to work on your mind and heart in those areas you've noted in the Going Forward section. Be honest about your desires and fears.

Notes for Small Groups:

- *Look for ways to put into practice the things you wrote in the Going Forward section. Talk with other group members about your ideas and commit to being accountable to one another.*
- *During the coming week, ask the Holy Spirit to continue to reveal truth to you from what you've read and studied.*
- *Before you start the next lesson, read 2 Corinthians 12:11—13:14. For more in-depth lesson preparation, read chapter 12, "Three to Get Ready!," in* Be Encouraged.

Readiness
(2 CORINTHIANS 12:11—13:14)

Before you begin …
- *Pray for the Holy Spirit to reveal truth and wisdom as you go through this lesson.*
- *Read 2 Corinthians 12:11—13:14. This lesson references chapter 12 in* Be Encouraged. *It will be helpful for you to have your Bible and a copy of the commentary available as you work through this lesson.*

Getting Started

From the Commentary

As Paul brought his letter to a close, his great love for the Corinthians constrained him to make one last appeal. He did not want his third visit to their church to be another painful experience for them and for him. He had opened his heart to them, explained his ministry, answered their accusations, and urged them to submit to the Word of God and obey the Lord.

—*Be Encouraged*, page 165

1. How did Paul appeal to the Corinthians in his conclusion? What can you learn about Paul's heart by the words he chose here? How was his plea more evidence of his own claim of apostleship?

2. Choose one verse or phrase from 2 Corinthians 12:11—13:14 that stands out to you. This could be something you're intrigued by, something that makes you uncomfortable, something that puzzles you, something that resonates with you, or just something you want to examine further. Write that here.

Going Deeper

From the Commentary

When we were children, how many times did we hear, "Shame on you!" from a parent or a neighbor? It is a good thing when people can be ashamed of their bad actions or attitudes. It is evidence of a hard heart and a calloused conscience when a guilty person no longer feels shame. "Were they ashamed when they had committed abomination? Nay, they were not at all ashamed, neither could they blush" (Jer. 6:15).

First, Paul shamed the Corinthians for their *lack of commendation* (2 Cor. 12:11–13). They should have been boasting about him instead of compelling him to boast. Instead, the Corinthians were boasting about the "super-apostles" (12:11 NIV), the Judaizers who had won their affection and were now running their church.

Was Paul inferior to these men? In no way! The Corinthians had seen Paul in action; in fact, they owed their very souls to him. He had done among them the miraculous signs that proved his apostleship (Heb. 2:1–4). He had persevered in his ministry at Corinth in spite of external persecution and internal problems. He had cost the church nothing. Paul used his subtle irony again when he wrote, "How were you inferior to the other churches, except that I was never a burden to you? Forgive me this wrong!" (2 Cor. 12:13 NIV).

—*Be Encouraged*, pages 165–66

3. How had the Corinthian believers become accustomed to their blessings? How can this be a negative thing for believers? How does this happen in today's church?

More to Consider: In spite of the difficulties involved, Paul had been faithful to visit the Corinthians; and now he was about to make his third visit (see 2 Cor. 13:1). Why did the Corinthians criticize Paul for changing his plans? (See 2 Cor. 11:3.) In what ways was Paul's relationship with the Corinthians like Christ's relationship with His followers?

From the Commentary

It is a tragic thing when children do not appreciate what their parents do for them. It is also a tragedy when God's children fail to appreciate what their "spiritual parents" do for them. What is the cause of this lack of appreciation? There were terrible sins in the church, and Paul wanted them judged and put away before he came for his visit. Otherwise, his visit would just be another painful experience.

Some of the church members were probably saying, "If Paul visits us again, he will just create more problems!" Paul made it clear that his desire was to *solve* problems and strengthen the church. Sins in the church must be faced honestly and dealt with courageously. To sweep them under the rug is to make matters worse. Sin in the church is like cancer in the human body: it must be cut out.

—*Be Encouraged*, page 167

4. What signs of cancer in the church did Paul point to in 2 Corinthians 12:19–21? Why would people in the church think Paul's visit might create more trouble than it might solve? When does the "status quo" become something to change rather than embrace? Why is there such resistance to this in churches?

From the History Books

In addition to our study of Jesus, modern churches spend a lot of time teaching about the spiritual heroes described in the Bible—people like Abraham and Isaac and Jacob. We also study the lives of New Testament characters, like Paul and Timothy. Learning about these biblical characters is critically important to our growth as Christians—their lives reveal much about our God and our own journeys of faith. Many contemporary churches supplement this teaching with stories of modern-day spiritual "heroes," people in the limelight for the way they display their faith in public forums—on the football field, in a television show, on the printed page.

5. How do we decide who is worthy of labeling a "spiritual hero" or "spiritual parent" today? It's a no-brainer when we're considering Scripture, but what about other historical men and women? What about modern-day heroes of the faith? What are the benefits of examining the lives of today's

believers in our efforts to better know God? What are the dangers? How can the Holy Spirit help us learn from men and women of integrity?

From the Commentary

In dealing with sin in a local church, we must have facts and not rumors. Paul quoted Deuteronomy 19:15, and we find parallels in Numbers 35:30 and Matthew 18:16, as well as 1 Timothy 5:19. The presence of witnesses would help to guarantee the truth about a matter, especially when the church members were at such variance with one another.

I have seen small disagreements in a church grow into large and complicated problems, only because the believers did not obey our Lord's directions. The pastor and congregation must not get involved in a matter until the individuals involved have sincerely sought a solution.

The Judaizers in the church had accused Paul of being a weak man (see 2 Cor. 10:7–11). Their approach to ministry was heavy-handed and dictatorial, while Paul's was gentle and humble (see 2 Cor. 1:24). Now Paul assured

them that he would show them how strong he could be—
if that is what it took to solve the problems. "I will not
spare!" was his warning, and he used a word that means
"to spare in battle."

—*Be Encouraged*, page 168

6. Read Matthew 18:15–20. How might these instructions from Jesus have
solved the Corinthians' problems? What did Paul say in this section of
2 Corinthians that revealed a change in his approach to the church? What
was Paul declaring war on?

From the Commentary

Second Corinthians 13:5–8 include an application of
the word *proof* that Paul used in verse 3. "You have been
examining me," wrote Paul, "but why don't you take time
to examine yourselves?" I have noticed in my ministry
that those who are quick to examine and condemn others
are often guilty of worse sins themselves. In fact, one way
to make yourself look better is to condemn somebody
else.

To begin with, Paul told the Corinthians that they should examine their hearts to see if they were really born again and members of the family of God.

—*Be Encouraged*, page 169

7. Paul took a bold stance here, asking the Corinthians to examine their own hearts. Specifically what did he want them to look for? (See Rom. 8:9, 16; 1 John 2:29; 3:9, 14; 1 John 5:4.) How can we apply these tests to our own lives to be certain that we are the children of God?

From the Commentary

In 2 Corinthians 13:7, Paul made it clear that he did not want the Corinthians to fail the test just to prove that he was right. Nor did he want them to live godly lives just so he could boast about them. He did not mind being despised and criticized for their sakes, so long as they were obeying the Lord. He was not concerned about his own reputation, for the Lord knew his heart; but he was concerned about their Christian character.

The important thing is the truth of the gospel and the Word of God (2 Cor. 13:8). Paul did not state here that it is impossible to attack the truth or hinder the truth, for these things were going on at that time in the Corinthian church. He was affirming that he and his associates wanted the truth to prevail, come what may, and that they were determined to further the truth, not obstruct it. In the end, God's truth will prevail, so why try to oppose it? "There is no wisdom nor understanding nor counsel against the Lord" (Prov. 21:30).

—*Be Encouraged*, pages 170–71

8. Read Proverbs 21:30. How does this verse line up with what Paul said in 2 Corinthians 13? What does it look like to "further the truth"? How do we know when the truth is being preached instead of something merely resembling the truth?

From the Commentary

Paul encouraged the Corinthians by his personal prayers on their behalf (2 Cor. 13:9). The word translated "wish" in the King James Version carries the meaning of "pray." Paul prayed for their *perfection*, which does not mean absolute sinless perfection, but "spiritual maturity." The word is part of a word family in the Greek that means "to be fitted out, to be equipped." As a medical term, it means "to set a broken bone, to adjust a twisted limb." It also means "to outfit a ship for a voyage" and "to equip an army for battle." In Matthew 4:21, it is translated "mending nets."

One of the ministries of our risen Lord is that of perfecting His people (Heb. 13:20–21). He uses the Word of God (2 Tim. 3:16–17) in the fellowship of the local church (Eph. 4:11–16) to equip His people for life and service. He also uses suffering as a tool to equip us (1 Peter 5:10). As Christians pray for one another (1 Thess. 3:10) and personally assist one another (Gal. 6:1, where "restore" is this same word *perfect*), the exalted Lord ministers to His church and makes them fit for ministry.

—*Be Encouraged*, page 171

9. Review 2 Corinthians 13:9–14. How did Paul encourage the Corinthians in this passage? In what ways did Paul teach the importance of community here? Is balanced Christian growth and ministry possible in isolation? Why or why not?

More to Consider: Read Jeremiah 1:7–10. How does this passage relate to Paul's challenges with the Corinthian church? What are the "weeds" that Paul had to pull up before he could plant a good crop?

From the Commentary

The closing benediction in 2 Corinthians 13:14 is one of the most beloved used in the church. It emphasizes the Trinity (see Matt. 28:19) and the blessings we can receive because we belong to God. *"The grace of our Lord Jesus Christ"* reminds us of His birth, when He became poor in order to make us rich (see 2 Cor. 8:9). The *"love of God"* takes us to Calvary, where God gave His Son as the sacrifice for our sins (John 3:16). The *"communion of the Holy Ghost"* reminds us of Pentecost, when the Spirit of God came and formed the church (Acts 2).

The Corinthian believers then, and all believers now, desperately needed the blessings of grace, love, and communion. The Judaizers then, and the cultists today, emphasized law instead of grace, exclusiveness instead of love, and independence rather than communion (fellowship). The competition in the Corinthian church, resulting in divisions, would have been solved if the people had only lived by God's grace and love.

The church is a miracle, and it can be sustained only by the miracle ministry of God. No amount of human skill, talents, or programs can make the church what it ought to be.

—*Be Encouraged*, pages 173–74

10. How does the closing in 2 Corinthians sum up Paul's heart for the Corinthians? What was Paul's ultimate message for the Corinthians? How did he live this out in his own life? How should we live it out today?

Looking Inward

Take a moment to reflect on all that you've explored thus far in this study of 2 Corinthians 12:11—13:14. Review your notes and answers and think about how each of these things matters in your life today.

> *Tips for Small Groups: To get the most out of this section, form pairs or trios and have group members take turns answering these questions. Be honest and as open as you can in this discussion, but most of all, be encouraging and supportive of others. Be sensitive to those who are going through particularly difficult times and don't press for people to speak if they're uncomfortable doing so.*

11. In what ways have you become accustomed to your blessings? How might this be a negative thing? What are some ways to embrace your blessings daily?

12. When have you taken time to examine your heart, motives, etc., as Paul instructed the Corinthians to do? What did you discover? What might you find today that you didn't find years ago? Why is it important to take stock of our hearts and minds in matters of faith?

13. What are some of the things you might need to tear down in yourself before you can build a better faith? How will you do that?

Going Forward

14. Think of one or two things that you have learned that you'd like to work on in the coming week. Remember that this is all about quality, not quantity. It's better to work on one specific area of life and do it well than to work on many and do poorly (or to be so overwhelmed that you simply don't try).

Do you want to reexamine your heart and mind in matters of faith? Be specific. Go back through 2 Corinthians 12:11—13:14 and put a star next to the phrase or verse that is most encouraging to you. Consider memorizing this verse.

Real-Life Application Ideas: Take some time this week to consider the people in your life who are "spiritual parents" or heroes of your faith. This probably will include biblical characters, but don't neglect those people in your family or friend circles who have had positive impacts on the development of your faith. If some of those people are still living, send each of them a note, thanking them for the role they've played in your life so far. Then take time to pray for them, that they might inspire others to grow spiritually as well. Finally, ask God to help you be a person of integrity who might inspire others to grow.

Seeking Help

15. Write a prayer below (or simply pray one in silence), inviting God to work on your mind and heart in those areas you've noted in the Going Forward section. Be honest about your desires and fears.

Notes for Small Groups:

- *Look for ways to put into practice the things you wrote in the Going Forward section. Talk with other group members about your ideas and commit to being accountable to one another.*

- *During the coming week, ask the Holy Spirit to continue to reveal truth to you from what you've read and studied.*

Summary and Review

Notes for Small Groups: This session is a summary and review of this book. Because of that, it is shorter than the previous lessons. If you are using this in a small-group setting, consider combining this lesson with a time of fellowship or a shared meal.

> *Before you begin …*
> - *Pray for the Holy Spirit to reveal truth and wisdom as you go through this lesson.*
> - *Briefly review the notes you made in the previous sessions. You will refer back to previous sections throughout this bonus lesson.*

Looking Back

1. Over the past eight lessons, you've examined Paul's second letter to the Corinthians. What expectations did you bring to this study? In what ways were those expectations met?

2. What is the most significant personal discovery you've made from this study?

3. What surprised you most about 2 Corinthians? What, if anything, troubled you?

Progress Report

4. Take a few moments to review the Going Forward sections of the previous lessons. How would you rate your progress for each of the things you chose to work on? What adjustments, if any, do you need to make to continue on the path toward spiritual maturity?

5. In what ways have you grown closer to Christ during this study? Take a moment to celebrate those things. Then think of areas where you feel you still need to grow and note those here. Make plans to revisit this study in a few weeks to review your growing faith.

Things to Pray About

6. Second Corinthians is a book about encouragement. As you reflect on Paul's letter, think about how you can be an encouragement to other believers. Then act on those thoughts.

7. The messages in 2 Corinthians include giving, ministry, persistence, faith, and spiritual integrity. Spend time praying for each of these topics.

8. Whether you've been studying this in a small group or on your own, there are many other Christians working through the very same issues you discovered when examining 2 Corinthians. Take time to pray for them, that God would reveal truth, that the Holy Spirit would guide you, and that each person might grow in spiritual maturity according to God's will.

A Blessing of Encouragement

Studying the Bible is one of the best ways to learn how to be more like Christ. Thanks for taking this step. In closing, let this blessing precede you and follow you into the next week while you continue to marinate in God's Word:

May God light your path to greater understanding as you review the truths found in 2 Corinthians and consider how they can help you grow closer to Christ.